Christ Is the Question

Wayne A. Meeks

WESTMINSTER
JOHN KNOX PRESS
LOUISVILLE · KENTUCKY

Scripture quotations from the New Revised Standard Version of the Bible are copyright © 1989 by the Division of Christian Education of the National Council of the Churches of Christ in the U.S.A. and are used by permission.

Scripture quotations from *The Revised English Bible*, © Oxford University Press and Cambridge University Press, 1989. Used by permission.

Book design by Sharon Adams
Cover design by Night & Day Design

First edition
Published by Westminster John Knox Press
Louisville, Kentucky

This book is printed on acid-free paper that meets the American National Standards Institute Z39.48 standard. ♾

PRINTED IN THE UNITED STATES OF AMERICA

06 07 08 09 10 11 12 13 14 15 — 10 9 8 7 6 5 4 3 2 1

Library of Congress Cataloging-in-Publication Data is on file at the Library of Congress, Washington, D.C.

ISBN-13: 978-0-664-22962-7
ISBN-10: 0-664-22962-X

Christ Is the Question

Luke Timothy Johnson

ὑπόμνησιν λαβὼν τῆς ἐν σοὶ ἀνυποκρίτου πίστεως

Contents

Preface

For many years students and friends have badgered or implored me to say something about Jesus. Until now I have shied away from this most central of issues for the New Testament scholar and for the Christian, because it seemed too difficult. Jesus, I replied to these entreaties, could be known only the way a black hole is known: by the effects, never directly. In spite of this conviction, questions about Jesus' identity, especially as posed by my friend Marinus de Jonge and my late friend, teacher, and colleague Hans Frei, have continued to nag me. The present book exists because Luke Timothy Johnson finally called my bluff. Five of the six chapters originated as lectures delivered at Emory University in the fall of 2004, when I served as the McDonald Visiting Distinguished Professor in the Study of the Person and Teachings of Jesus. I am grateful to Luke for not taking no for an answer, to him and his colleagues and other longtime friends in Atlanta for care and hospitality beyond all expectations, and to Alonzo L. McDonald and Suzanne M. McDonald for their kindness and the

McDonald Agape Foundation for making it all possible. Cyril O'Regan and Dale Martin read chapters 1 and 2, and their suggestions led to significant improvement. For their help and enduring friendship, many thanks indeed.

Three of the lectures were repeated at Williams College in the Croghan Bicentennial Lectures series in February and March 2005; special thanks to William R. Darrow, chair of the Department of Religion and Jackson Professor of Religion, for the invitation to be part of that exciting community in the spring term of 2005. Parts of chapters 2 and 3 draw on the W. K. Pritchett Lecture for 1999 at the University of California, Berkeley; the Alexander Robertson lecture of 2001 at the University of Glasgow; the inaugural Nils Alstrup Dahl Lecture at the University of Oslo in 2003; and the Croghan Lecture, April 6, 2004, at Williams College.[1] Chapter 5, in a slightly shorter version and under a different title, has been published in the *Yale Review*. Chapter 1 is entirely new and chapter 2 substantially augmented and rewritten. However, I have retained much of the oral style of the lectures throughout, and I have avoided the temptation to add a large apparatus of notes—even though as a result much of my obvious indebtedness to other scholars must go unacknowledged.

Thanks to Westminster John Knox Press, with which I have had a long and happy connection, and especially to Donald McKim for agreeing to make a book of these musings. Most of all I thank all those students whose curiosity, daring, new ideas, persistent stubbornness, and loyalty have made teaching for me a way of life and a way of learning. Their names are too numerous to mention; Luke Timothy Johnson must stand in for all of them as *primus inter pares*, as I dedicate the book to him with affection and gratitude.

Chapter One

Answers and Questions

We've all seen the bumper stickers and the billboards. In some parts of the United States they're inescapable: "Christ [or Jesus] is the Answer." I confess that when I see these signs my silent response is something like, "But what's the question?" In fact I have known people who made a game of inventing impious questions to which "Christ" could be the answer (such as, "What's a six-letter word that means 'I just dropped a rock on my foot'?"). It is understandable that many non-Christians are offended by the slogan; it bespeaks a careless and superficial kind of proselytizing. But why do I, and many other Christians I know, also find the slogan offensive, or at least silly? I used to think it was only a kind of snobbishness on my part, a matter of taste and class and an intellectual's pride, but the more I have considered the issue—and I have spent my entire professional career, not to mention much of my childhood, trying to make sense of the Bible—the more I am confirmed in my judgment. Christ is the question, not the answer.

Of course I can understand why a convert to Christianity, or a maturing Christian newly discovering the depth dimensions of a casually adopted faith, might in all innocence and sincerity sum up his or her experience with the phrase, "Christ is the answer." Used that way, it belongs to the same genre as Augustine's rather more eloquent (and trinitarian) confession, "You have made us for yourself; our heart is restless until it rests in you."[1] It would be spoken with a strong sense that the phrase hid more than it revealed, that it pointed to a complex story of seeking and finding, of struggle and release, of self-discovery and self-commitment. If we pursued a real conversation about the experience, the shallowness of the slogan would be swallowed up by the depths of the personal story signaled by it.

The slogan on the billboard is another matter. It enshrines shallowness and exploits it in order to sell Jesus. Like so much of the public discourse about religion in the United States in recent decades, this and similar slogans represent the commodification of religion. Jesus becomes another brand to be marketed. As a brand of shampoo promises the answer to frizzy hair, a detergent brand the answer to unbright laundry, a new model car the answer to loneliness and (by innuendo) sexual longing, so Jesus is the answer to—what? Whatever you wish. Indeed Jesus has become whatever you wish, an all-purpose brand, the answer to all needs, desires, fantasies, and speculations.

In the Bible, the questions God asks are often more important—or at least clearer—than the answers that are provided. To Adam, "Where are you?" "Who told you that you were naked?" To Cain, "Where is your brother Abel?" "What are you doing here, Elijah?" To Isaiah, "Whom shall I send, and who will go for us?" "Amos, what do you see?" And, from Jesus, "But who do *you* say that I am?"

This book is about the questions that surround the

identity of Jesus—mainly in the context of American Protestantism, but I do not write either as a theologian or as an analyst of American culture. I am rather a New Testament exegete and a historian of earliest Christianity— fields that many believed, a century ago, would surely provide us with clear and reliable answers. Instead, I and other scholars who have spent their lives studying the documents and environment of early Christianity find that the more we study, the more questions we have. One of my reasons for writing this book is to sketch out very simply why that has been the case. Another reason for writing is to explain my conviction that having so many questions may be a good thing, not a cause for lamentation. Indeed, many Christians I know who have lived long and deeply in the faith also have more questions than answers and, even more surprisingly, believe that questions may be more expressive of their faith and better pointers to the ground of their confidence than "answers."

The Many Faces of Jesus

The first and most obvious question to be asked about Jesus Christ in our culture is, "Which Jesus?" "Which Christ?" Is it the "gentle Jesus, meek and mild," of Victorian sentimentality, or the "touchdown Jesus" that many football fans have seen in the larger-than-life mosaic that presides, from their perspective, over the Notre Dame stadium? Is it the blonde, blue-eyed young man of Warner Sallman's *Head of Christ*, which remains the nearest thing to an icon in white Protestant churches and homes, or the black Jesus who has appeared in more and more black churches? Is it the athletic youth of "muscular Christianity" once popularized by the YMCA, or is it the bleeding and emaciated body suspended from the crucifix in most

Catholic churches? Is it the "Man Nobody Knows," whose servanthood is a model for business success, like the Rotary Club's motto, "He profits most who serves best"? Or the revolutionary savior of the working classes admired by Eugene Debs and his followers in the early labor movement? Is it the feminist Jesus, breaking the rules of gendered society to call female disciples, or even the womanist Jesus, embodying in himself (herself?) the traits society calls "feminine," or is it rather the stern upholder of patriarchy as foundation of "family values"?[2]

The multiple identities of Jesus in American culture are not a new phenomenon. The very first Europeans to arrive in the Western Hemisphere brought with them varying conceptions—and uses—of Christ, and every succeeding generation has added new images of Jesus, reflecting the variety of imported and homegrown American culture. Two recent books, by Richard Wightman Fox and Stephen Prothero (both cited in note 2), have described some of the immense variety of ways Americans have imagined, worshiped, co-opted, parodied, or feared Jesus Christ. As one of them sums up, "Four centuries of Jesus in America: so many Christs, so many cultural incarnations, secular and religious alike."[3]

"Cultural incarnations" are neither new nor peculiar to America. If there is anything unique about the American Jesus, it is only the number and variety of his images—and their ubiquity in a public life that is functionally almost wholly secular. But whenever and wherever followers of Jesus have spoken of "incarnation," that has necessarily entailed an incarnation in culture—the culture of a particular time and place and set of social forms. How could it be otherwise? To be human is to be in culture, and if the Son of God, as the fathers at Nicaea required Christians to confess, "was made man," then he was made a person whose identity must be expressed through cultural practices. (We'll talk more about that in subsequent chapters.) No wonder, then, that no matter how early we go back in the history of believers in Jesus the Christ, we find a variety of ways of expressing who the believers thought he was. From the very beginning not only were there different conceptions of Jesus' identity, but those conceptions frequently conflicted with one other. Sometimes the conflicts were severe enough that some believers separated themselves from others, and when compromises were worked out, often they had to be enforced by external power—at Nicaea in the fourth century, for the first time, by the power of the Roman emperor himself, and since then by a vast array of overt and subtle forms of persuasion and coercion. Resentment of that kind of enforcement and resistance to it are hallmarks of the sensibility we call "modern"—and of course are deeply woven into the fabric of America's own national memory and sentiment. We relish free choice, but how do we choose among the many Jesuses?

The question imposed by the variety of Christ's cultural identities, "Which one shall we believe?" thus pushes us toward a deeper and more troubling question. Is there *one* Christ behind or within all these many ways of imagining him, or have we only an infinitely expandable multitude of culturally contingent icons? It is easy to see that many of the images are projections of the hopes, aspirations, or prejudices of groups or individuals; are they *all*?

These unsettling questions, together with the notion that, if we really set our minds to it, we could get to the bottom of them all and find answers on which all reasonable people could agree, can almost be said to define what it means to be "modern" in matters of religion. And, because we are moderns, we must find out the truth for ourselves. We have learned not to trust authorities—or at least that is what we like to tell ourselves. The creeds are an antique survival. The Jesus they confess has very little obviously in common with the Jesus we meet on television or in the preaching of our most popular evangelists. Even in those churches which do still recite one of the traditional creeds, at least on Communion Sundays, the familiar words can hardly be said to settle the questions for most of us, and the conflicts they once were crafted to pacify seem very far from us. We can hardly imagine blood being spilled, as once it was, over the question whether Christ is of *the same* substance with the Father or only of *like* substance with him. The former language may be comforting to those of us raised in liturgical churches, but if someone were to prefer the alternative, different by only one letter in Greek but once a matter of life and death, we would only shrug and perhaps recall Gibbon's sarcasm about "the furious contests which the difference of a single diphthong excited."[4] The creed's language is familiar (albeit for fewer and fewer among us), but the more it remains the same, the more it changes. It answers questions that belong to a different world, not ours. The authority that proclaims it is not what it used to be.[5] We, every man and woman of us, will decide for ourselves the truth about Jesus. How will we go about that?

History to the Rescue?

By the end of the nineteenth century it seemed obvious to a great many modern Christians that there was only one reliable way to answer the question, Who was Jesus *really*? That way was the way of historical research. To say that Jesus belonged to history was not, of course, new. The ancient baptismal creed declared that he was "crucified under Pontius Pilate," thus pinning the central salvific action of the Christian narrative to a singular moment in political history. That claim created serious issues for early Christian apologists, trying to make the new faith plausible to the philosophically literate—indeed, those issues continued to exercise the reasoning of Christian theologians in every generation. As Gotthold Ephraim Lessing famously summed up the problem, which had taken on new life in the eighteenth century, "accidental truths of history can never become the proof of necessary truths of reason."[6] But the apologists were happy to insist that this "scandal" of locating God's ultimate revelation in an event of recent memory was precisely what separated the Christian claim from the "fables" and "myths" of the Greek and Roman gods. However intractable the problem of uniting the universal with the particular might seem, it was a problem that succeeding generations of Christian theologians, themselves trained in the schools of classical philosophy, attacked with zest. In time they achieved a delicate synthesis of reason and revelation, of nature and grace, that might have to be revisited again and again, but which by the late Middle Ages seemed quite secure. By the time of Lessing, however, a growing number of Western European thinkers were pointing out that "pagans" were not the only ones capable of myth-making. Christians, too, had sometimes been guilty of fabulating. Certainly the Protestant Reformers had been happy to point out the myths and fables that the papacy, in their view, had introduced to maintain its own power. But by the eighteenth century there were some who dared to say that the biblical writers themselves might have used myths to convey their message.

In 1835 and 1836 a young lecturer at the Protestant seminary in the German university town of Tübingen published a two-volume book that used the concept of myth as both a literary and a philosophical tool for "critically analyzing" the "life of Jesus" portrayed in the Gospels. The publication caused an uproar; the young man, David Friedrich Strauss, was fired and was never able afterwards to hold a permanent academic post. The questions he had raised in his book, however, would not go away. In 1864 Strauss published a smaller *Life of Jesus*, this one adapted "for the German people." By that time the invention of high-speed printing presses had made books an affordable commodity and created a large market for popularizations of current intellectual issues. Strauss's book was a best seller—as, just a year earlier, Ernest Renan's equally modern, though less well-informed, *Life of Jesus* had been in France. No less a literary figure than George Eliot (Marian Evans) translated Strauss's earlier book for the English-speaking world, where it caused a sensation only slightly smaller than it had in Germany. The popular version also found an English publisher promptly, and Renan's, too, quickly appeared and gained a long-lasting popularity in English. The determination to answer the Jesus question with the tools of modern historiography had burst out of the academic closet. The diverse and rapidly growing assortment of writers whom Albert Schweitzer would gather into the Life of Jesus movement, in his magisterial and delightfully opinionated history of their work, had taken center stage.[7]

The long, complex intellectual struggles represented by the few examples I have named here effected a sea change in religious sensibilities in European and American Christendom—initially almost exclusively among Protestants but later also among Catholics, and indeed among both believers and nonbelievers. Talk about the "historical Jesus" and the flow of new books with that phrase or something like it in their titles is so common-place now that we forget how radically the new questions departed from the great theological debates of the earlier centuries. Both the innocent-sounding words, "historical" and "Jesus," pointed to new ways of thinking. The revolutionary thinkers of the Renaissance, of the Reformation, and of the Enlightenment raised questions above all about God, not about Jesus. The human Jesus was taken for granted. Insofar as questions were raised about him, they were on the abstract level of trinitarian theology: How could the Godhead assume humanity? How could the particular embody the universal? How could the temporal manifest the eternal? No one thought these questions could be answered by *biography*. In the nineteenth century, Jesus became quite literally the question, the center of popular religion, and the uncontested focus for pious curiosity. Equally novel was the conviction that the way to answer the Jesus question was by doing *history*—specifically, by writing a modern, historical biography of Jesus. More important, the whole notion of history and of how to do it was quite different from what it had been.

Although these two novelties, the new centrality of the human Jesus and the new history, came together dramatically in the nineteenth century to transform Protestant thinking, both changes had begun much earlier—in the Renaissance humanism of the fourteenth century and, even earlier, in some late-medieval currents of piety and thought. Francis of Assisi and the Franciscan theologians after him, as Louis Dupré explains, first upset the "axiomatic primacy of the universal" in the church's doctrine of incarnation, by introducing an individualistic devotion to Jesus of Nazareth.[8] The emotional attachment to Jesus' human experiences which the Franciscan devotion entailed was conveyed to ordinary worshipers by popular preaching and, in a different way, by the "natu-ralism" of Renaissance paintings of Jesus. One of the most popular devotional books of the fourteenth century was *Meditations on the Life of Christ* by the Franciscan John of Caulibus (Giovanni de' Cauli'; the book was once falsely attributed to the much more famous Franciscan, St. Bonaventure). The *Meditations* invite the worshiper to empathize with Jesus' feelings and sufferings, "for He had real and susceptible flesh like all other humans."[9] The art historian Leo Steinberg has argued that such Franciscan-inspired sentiments profoundly influenced the way in which Renaissance artists, both north and south of the Alps, came to portray Christ—even extending to a new and surprising emphasis on the genitalia of both the Christ child and of the dead Christ. Here the manhood of Jesus was celebrated indeed. What was happening, Stein-berg argues, was not just a shift to "realism" in art, but a new way of symbolizing what was religiously significant about Jesus.[10]

Not only the new religious concentration on the human Jesus, but also the new concept of history had its roots in the Renaissance. This "rebirth" of humanism beginning in fourteenth-century Italy was essentially a rediscovery of classical models from Greek and Roman antiquity, in literature, in art and architecture, in philoso-phy and rhetoric, and in science. Rediscovering the glo-ries of the past became central to the task of learning to live fully in the present. The humanist thinkers set their minds to master those tools that would enable them to find and to analyze critically the traces of the past and to bring it into their own time. Manuscripts of the classical writers' works were diligently collected and edited. The techniques of the Greek grammarians, such as the textual critics of Alexandria and Antioch, were redeployed in the search for the most authentic voices of Plato and Aristotle, Homer, Aeschylus, and Euripides. Forgeries were detected (and new ones created); the structure of language, both grammatical and rhetorical, became the object of new study and new imitation. Sculptors and architects labored to excavate and measure the ruins of Rome's great monuments. Inevitably the humanists would apply the same techniques to the texts and monuments of Christianity—sometimes with startling results. In 1440 Lorenzo Valla proved that the document by which the papal states had justified their domination of the area of Rome, the "Donation of Constantine," was an eighth-century forgery. What other fundamental texts might come under suspicion? What was one to make of the divergences among the thousands of manuscripts of the Greek and Latin Bible? In time the vast scholarly energy unleashed by the Renaissance would produce new critical editions—most famous being the New Testaments of Stephanus and Erasmus—which would have enormous impact on the movements of reform in the sixteenth century and after.

For all their infatuation with the past, however, the sense of history that drove the Renaissance scholars was not yet modern, and in an important respect it was, from the modern perspective, only protohistorical. For those scholars of the fourteenth to the sixteenth centuries, the past was not a foreign country; the classical values were *their* values. They could not merely observe the past, they could inhabit it. Their very humanism (and their Neoplatonism) insisted that essential nature did not change. When we read the letters of Seneca or of Cicero, they felt, we might well imagine that they were addressed to us. But that would change. The more one learned of the past, the more inescapable became the cumulative evidence that the men (and women, though they were not often noticed) of past ages were not like us. Already in the sixteenth century, Montaigne observed that those differences were so great that it was silly to expect answers from the past to questions of the present. The critical practice of the Renaissance had produced a questioning temperament that eventually would undermine some of its own most precious assumptions, producing in Montaigne's time a rise of skepticism—ironically, itself seen as a revival of an ancient movement identified with Pyrrhon of the fourth century BCE. The idealism that undergirded the humanist's confidence in the essential sameness of humanity, the assumption that what is real is the universal, was itself coming under attack.[11]

The Renaissance preoccupation with rediscovering the past was a powerful impetus toward the modern conception of history, but the new, skeptical mood would twist this quest into something altogether different. If Dupré is right, some of the most important elements of that skepticism originated in that same rich Franciscan soil which produced the popular Jesus piety. It was Franciscan thinkers and writers, especially the Britons Duns Scotus and William of Ockham, who would produce in the philosophical world the revolution we call nominalism.[12] If with the nominalists we begin to question whether universals are real or only "names" (*nomina*), then we have set foot on the path that leads to the empiricism of eighteenth-century science: only those things are real that we can observe and measure. Warned by Ockham not to multiply assumed causes beyond those necessary to explain any particular phenomenon we are trying to describe ("Ockham's Razor"), we may be on the way to the position attributed, in a famous but possibly apocryphal story, to the great mathematician of the late eighteenth century,

Pierre-Simon Laplace. Before the French Revolution, Laplace had written a grand treatise on the mathematics of "celestial mechanics." Years later, according to the story, Napoleon asked him where God fit into his explanation of the planets' orbits, to which Laplace replied, "Sire, I had no need of that hypothesis." No, if the universe is a machine, then if we are clever enough we can explain its operations from the laws of mechanics. Nature can be understood without assuming "supernatural" causes. The English Deists had already arrived at this conclusion, but they sought to save the Christian doctrine of creation by keeping God in the picture at the beginning: God made the great machine and wound it up, but thereafter it ran on its own, and God was unemployed.

In the age of science, the history of human events must also yield to explanations that eschew "supernatural" interventions. Not only did such a mechanistic conception of events call into question the notion of miracles, which had seemed so necessary an element of the biblical stories, it also played havoc with the doctrine of the incarnation, which portrayed Christ's human life as God's supreme intervention in the fallen world. If not that, then what was the meaning of Christ for those—the majority—of the new thinkers who still saw themselves as Christians and wrestled intensely with these questions in order to find a rationally satisfying basis for their religion? For many of them, God was still to be found active in the world, but neither in the mode of ancient classical thought, in which the gods were part of nature, nor in the paradoxical mode of traditional Christian theology, in which God utterly transcended the world but engaged himself in it to create, to chastise, and to redeem. Rather, one must look for God precisely in the divinity of reason itself. As God was pure reason and pure goodness, so God was to be found reflected within human reasoning and the human conscience. Was not Jesus, then, the supreme instance of that God-consciousness which, in his own day, manifested the divine reason and virtue against all human superstition, ignorance, and vice? To know Jesus fully, then, to think his thoughts and to learn his teachings, was to see into the mind of God. As the biography of every genius was illuminating, so the true story of Jesus must be the supreme enlightenment.[13]

Historicism in Crisis

We have been following two lines of development. One was a narrowing of religious focus, in the Western Christian world, to the human life of Jesus as the central issue of belief and disbelief. The other was the emergence of a new way of understanding the past, a writing of history that tried to emulate the objectivity of the physical sciences. In the nineteenth century the two became sometimes opponents, sometimes uneasy partners. New forms of piety and new forms of skepticism were in collision, but believers and skeptics tended to agree on one thing: the central issues had to do with Jesus of Nazareth. Even though Jesus-piety typically insisted that the knowledge that counted was a matter of the heart rather than of the mind, every believer was convinced that the facts about Jesus' life in ancient Galilee and Judaea were important—whether those facts were simply obvious in a naive reading of the Gospel texts or had to be discovered and confirmed through the diligence of scientific history.

Scientific history—that was the new thing. The most visible success of the new ways of thinking was to be found in the triumph of modern science. Because the new science, already in the seventeenth century, had focused its efforts not only on understanding but on controlling nature, it gave birth to a technology that literally transformed (and is still transforming) the world in which ordinary people live. Those results were eventually inescapable. Inevitably historians would fall under the spell of that "physics envy" of which John Gaddis has accused both social scientists and his historian colleagues who copy them.[14] What they envied and tried to emulate was the objectivity that the scientific method promised. The new science depended upon precise, empirical, and repeatable observation, followed by inductive generalization. Thinking about the observed facts produced hypotheses, but only to be tested by new observations. Only in that way could one move from fact to theory— and not, as in the old science, from theory to fact. If everything was done properly, anyone following the same procedure would find the same results, would draw the same conclusions, because those results were a reflection of what was really out there in nature. If one were going to build an Eiffel Tower or a Brooklyn Bridge, one must know the tensile strength of the particular kind of steel employed. Its value could not depend upon opinion or feeling; it could not vary according to which engineer one asked; it could never be deduced from the Ideal Form of Steel, not even if Socrates himself were helping us to think about it. Similarly, in scientific history we are not after what we would like to have happened, nor what our hearts tell us must have happened, nor what "always happens," but what really happened. The values of the ancient historians—to tell a rhetorically elegant and morally edifying story, to exhibit the abiding truths of humanity in the flux of time and culture—no longer cut any ice. The historian's job, as one of scientific history's most famous practitioners put it, is to tell "how it really was."[15]

There is no denying the monumental success of scientific history-writing, or its importance in enhancing the ways we understand ourselves and our world: more impressive than the Eiffel Tower and the Brooklyn Bridge, more important than even the electron tube, the airplane, and—dare I say it?—the computer. Nevertheless, there was a worm in Newton's apple and a crack in the mirror of history. No one took Nietzsche very seriously when he said, "There are no facts; there are only interpretations," but that remark was more prescient than even he probably could have guessed.[16] In order to understand the problem, we have to go back for a moment to that pivotal thinker at the birth of modernity, René Descartes.

The crisis of skepticism that had erupted in the mid-sixteenth century, as we saw above, led Montaigne to doubt that history could discover in the past any lessons at all. The human story was a story of constant change. Not only were the people of the past different from those of the present, every individual was different from every other. When Montaigne turned his gaze within himself, he found no stable core of being, but constant flux. Yet that turn within seemed to him to promise the only hope of true self-knowledge, even though it threatened to undermine the foundations of all dependable knowledge of the world. For Descartes as well, the key turn was a turn within, but boldly intending a result the very opposite of Montaigne's skepticism. By a remarkable topsy-turvy, Descartes transformed the doubts of the skeptics into a new kind of philosophical foundation, aiming, as Dupré says, "to restore the foundations of human knowledge by converting moral uncertainty into philosophical doubt and doubt itself into a method for attaining certainty."[17] The doubter of everything dubious must at least believe that he himself exists. Thinking, at least, is real: "I think, therefore I am." And then upon that narrow foundation the thinker proceeds to reconstruct the world, for if I, the thinking self, exist, then that thinking, even though cast in the form of the most radical doubt, restores confidence in the mind's ability to reflect the real. Science finds its needed foundation, for I can form concepts that accurately represent the world.

That required objectivity is purchased, as it turns out, at a very high cost. That wonderful "I" somehow is made to stand outside the whole "objective" world and controls the whole show. "A representation of reality now has to be constructed. As the notion of 'idea' migrates from [its Platonic meaning, the universal that alone is real] . . . to things 'in the mind,' so the order of ideas ceases to be something we *find* and becomes something we *build*."[18] The objectivity of the world—which for Descartes includes the objectification of his own body—depends upon a radically new subjectivity. In this new rationalism, that thinking substance, the individual, disembodied self, becomes the measure and judge of all things. According to Charles Taylor, John Locke took the next, decisive step toward that punctiliar notion of the self that has come to dominate modernity, by making the very process of knowing almost mechanistic, depending upon a mind that is both disengaged and controlling and thus itself an objective thing. Thus Locke's epistemology brings about "one of the great paradoxes of modern philosophy," namely, that the disengagement and objectification "helped to create a picture of the human being . . . from which the last vestiges of subjectivity seem to have been expelled," even though this "severe outlook" is based on "radical subjectivity."[19] In our own time that self would come to seem most fragile, ill suited to the command position assigned it by the Cartesian foundationalism, its principal virtue, that clear, controlling rationality attributed to it by Locke, a cruel delusion. Descartes taught us a sublime confidence in our own subjective rationality: any idea that appears to our minds as clear and obvious, as *évidente*, is certainly true. In the twentieth century a number of things happened that have led us to mistrust that confidence.

Among the new ways of thinking was one that, though later than the others to penetrate our modern consciousness, perhaps struck most deeply of all at our bedrock certainty that we knew *how to know* the world around us. That was the revolution in modern physics itself. The mechanical universe of Newton had to yield to the quantum mechanics of Einstein; the mathematics of certainty gave way to the Heisenberg principle of uncertainty at the heart of physical reality. Noticing this fluidity in the central concepts of physics, the "hardest" science of them all, philosophers of science began to point out that the scientific picture of the universe was not so objective after all. That thinking self which guaranteed the foundations of knowledge was a contingent self, rooted in a particular culture and a particular history, a mind shaped fundamentally by cultural categories including language itself.[20]

The dethroning of the sovereign, individual mind was helped along by a second revolution that shocked modernist sensibilities even earlier, the revolution in psychology. The beginning of the twentieth century marked the time when the social sciences were separating themselves from philosophy and finding their own specific ways of learning as *sciences*—of sociology, anthropology, economics, political science, as well as psychology. Of these none transformed the popular imagination so much as did Freud's explorations of the unconscious. In one sense the Freudian introspection was the culmination of that atomizing of the inward-looking individual self inaugurated by

Descartes and enhanced by John Locke's instrumental rationalism. On the other hand, the Freudian map of the unconscious undermined forever the Cartesians' solemn confidence in the self's happy rationality. At the "depths" of the self was more chaos than even Montaigne had feared, primal urges that society had forced us to repress in the name of its survival and our own, but which had a way of leaking into our thoughts and activities as "Freudian slips," or as "projections." These repressed forces insidiously affected our beliefs and our actions, and all our fine Cartesian rationality, Freud taught us, was shot through with "rationalization" of the unconscious determinants.

Several other developments have helped to break the nerve of modernism at the very moment of its triumph. Speaking quite broadly, we could call them an ideological revolution. Marxism in its various forms was preeminent in advancing this modern use of the term "ideology," pointing to ways in which institutions and beliefs and "spiritual" entities masked the real sources of power, which were economic and crudely material. A great many people who did not accept the Marxist system nevertheless had to agree that a lot of our public pieties concealed deep inequities in our society, that ceremonial platitudes more often than not celebrated relations of power that seemed "natural" only to those who were on top. We have already seen how scientific history, when it did its job best, might itself find in the land of the dead not our familiar values, but a strange culture that challenged our ways of reasoning and behaving. Even more, the new sciences of ethnography and anthropology, though in early days they sailed in the company of the exploiters and missionaries of the newly discovered lands, came slowly to make us aware of countless ways of living which were not just "savage" and "primitive," but certainly different from our own and which might—horrible thought!—do some things better. "Cultural relativism" entered our vocabulary: the notion that what we unthinkingly believe and what we most naturally do depend on where and when we live, on how we have been socialized. As Sakini put it, in *Teahouse of the August Moon*, "Pornography question of geography."[21] All these developments (and more) led in the mid-twentieth century to what Paul Ricoeur called "the hermeneutics of suspicion."[22] That radical doubt that Descartes had harnessed to lay the foundations of truth had slipped out of its safe niche, like some repressed primal drive in a Freudian dream, and battered the foundation to pieces.[23]

The Modern Jesus after Modernism

With the foundations of scientific history thus threatened, as it were, from within, what was to become of that "quest of the historical Jesus," which, as we have seen, depended on modern historicism for its confidence? It is time to look more closely at some of its assumptions, to see why, despite its perennially renewed optimism in recent generations, it failed to achieve its objectives. In the next chapter we examine its romancing of novelty, as time and again some accidental discovery of an ancient text or an ancient idea seemed to furnish at last the long-lost key to the unsuspected secret truth about Jesus: magical spells, Egyptian papyri, the Dead Sea Scrolls, the Nag Hammadi horde, and many others, each the celebrity find for a generation. We will learn to be wary of that irresistible tendency of the modernist mind to invent a name to pull together the disparate phenomena in our field of observation—Apocalypticism, Hellenism, Gnosticism—and then to treat the name as if it were something real, a cause that can *explain* distantly perceived effects. Above all, I suggest that a major reason why scientific history's search for the real Jesus failed was that we were all working with an inadequate model of human selfhood. I argue that we may get further by adopting a model of the self that is even more modern: a model of personal identity as a social and transactional process. It is a model developed by psychologists and others from the observation that each of us comes to know "who I am," not just by sitting and thinking about myself, but, beginning in earliest childhood, by responding to other persons who respond to me. My personal identity is not a hidden essence to be discovered, but an emerging story to be lived and told, in a language not private to me but shared with all who live in the culture into which I am born. Using that model will not get us to the *real* Jesus, either, but it may help us to escape from the subjective idealism and romanticism that have warped all our recent images of him.

I want to persuade the reader that, even if historians cannot produce a reliable biography of the real Jesus, we can describe the process by which Jesus became that personage who *made history*. Understanding that process may be more important for us, even more interesting, than constructing yet another "historical" Jesus. The earliest followers of Jesus struggled to find appropriate images to say who Jesus was—to themselves and to others. Their struggle was a self-involving process, for it was at the same time a struggle for the identity of a new movement. It was at heart an interpretive process, both in the broad sense that the work of forming an identity always both interprets the world and interprets one's own being in it, and in the specific sense that sacred texts and traditions about their meaning were centrally involved. Outlining some of the main parts of that struggle is the project of our third chapter. Comparisons with similar processes that can be seen at work in the Dead Sea Scrolls help us to understand what was going on.

Our fourth chapter focuses on the interpreter of Jesus whom we know best, because writings by him, by his disciples, and about him occupy a third of the pages of the New Testament: the apostle Paul. More clearly than any of the other interpreters we know, Paul understood that to become a follower of Jesus meant to live in a new way—in a world made new. Further, he saw that what made that difference was not to be discerned so readily in the story of how Jesus lived as in how he died. We ask what Paul meant when he told one of his most obstreperous congregations that the only thing that mattered—and at the same time the most mysterious thing of all—was "the word of the cross." When the apostle Paul speaks of the *logos* of the cross, he means more than just talking about the crucifixion of Jesus. He means that, for those who have been seized by "the faith of Jesus Christ," the very logic of reality has changed. That change can be expressed only by indirection, by metaphor. And thus begins an imperious, subversive narrative that seeks to incorporate the whole human story into itself and which, as a consequence, never rests, is never finished.

Frustrated by the scarcity of assured results from the complicated history we have been rehearsing here, we may be tempted to say, "Why not be satisfied with just what the Bible says about Jesus?" Unfortunately that is not so simple. To help us to understand why it is not, the fifth chapter reflects on the phrase we hear so frequently these days, "The Bible clearly teaches. . . ." Nine times out of ten when I hear this, whatever the alleged teaching that follows, I am moved to respond, "No, it doesn't," or, perhaps more charitably, "How do you know?" Here one of the principles most sacred to the Protestant Reformers is at stake, the "clarity" or "transparency" of Scripture. I argue that that doctrine is being fundamentally misused in discourse that tries to pry "answers" to complex moral questions directly out of (carefully selected) verses of Scripture. When someone says, "The Bible clearly teaches . . . ," we can usually be sure that an attempt is being made to co-opt the Bible's authority in order to foreclose argument on a topic on which good persons, including good Christians, reasonably disagree. Can we arrive at a *right* interpretation of the Bible—or must that possibility await the day when, as Paul says, "I shall know as I have been known"?

The final chapter takes up a question that, living in the twenty-first century, we cannot evade: Is Jesus the *last* word? Traditionally, Christians have insisted that the revelation of God in Jesus Christ is "unsurpassable." In what sense ought we still to affirm that? How do we say it to a Muslim? To a Buddhist? The Christian will affirm that no other story can be substituted for the story of Jesus, but that is not the same thing as saying that God has nothing further to say. Given the malleability of Jesus' identity that we have witnessed in the history of Christendom, where can we say the incarnate Word becomes *finally* known? When we remember how often our efforts to convert the world have been entangled with several kinds of imperialism, are we sure that God really wants everybody to be a Christian?

Chapter Two

Does Anybody Know My Jesus?

Between Dogma and Romanticism

In the previous chapter we saw how questions about the identity of Jesus became central to religious sensibilities in the modern period of European and—even more— American Christianity. And we saw the inordinate hope placed in scientific history to answer those questions, and the confusion that resulted more recently when those hopes were frustrated by a widespread disillusionment with the promises of historicism itself. In this chapter we look a little more closely at some of the particular problems with the "quest of the historical Jesus." Can anything be salvaged from the ruins of that movement? Are there, at the very least, lessons to be learned from its failure?

Old and New Quests for the Historical Jesus

Albert Schweitzer, in the final chapter of his history of "life of Jesus research," wrote what sounds like its obituary: "There is nothing more negative than the result of the critical study of the Life of Jesus."[1] That judgment had not deterred Schweitzer from writing his own life of Jesus, which he published five years earlier.[2] The temptation was apparently irresistible, and continues to be so down to the present. The Life of Jesus movement has had more lives than a feral tomcat. Its revivals are the more remarkable when we consider the eminent scholars who have tried to bury it. Among them were Rudolf Bultmann, the most influential New Testament scholar of the twentieth century, and the century's most important Protestant theologian, Karl Barth.

As a student, Bultmann had been trained in the optimistic liberal theology of the late nineteenth-century academy, as well as the strict philological and historical science of modern exegesis. He experienced very directly the collapse of the liberals' optimistic temperament in the social disruptions that shattered European confidence during and after World War I. The Swiss scholar Karl Barth, then teaching in the German university of Bonn, reacted even more vehemently to that experience. In their different ways, both Barth and Bultmann found in Søren Kierkegaard's "Attack upon Christendom," in the Danish writer's offbeat, quasi-poetic, often ironic publications (one of which actually bore this title), a way to a new, "dialectical" theology that could break through the cultural captivity of church and academy alike.[3] As the Nazi Party began in the 1930s to consolidate its stranglehold on both church and university, that cultural captivity took a bizarre and frightening turn. Barth, driven out of Germany, returned to his native Switzerland, where he criticized the German situation from across the border, and gradually turned from Kierkegaard's existentialism to a profoundly traditional and broadly historical, but radically rethought "Church Dogmatics."[4] Bultmann remained in his chair of New Testament studies at Marburg and committed his theological grounding more and more to the existentialist philosophy launched by Kierkegaard and represented at Marburg by Martin Heidegger (as one who had supported the Nazi Party up until 1933, Heidegger was Bultmann's political opposite, but philosophically he remained his primary informant).

Neither Barth's theology nor Bultmann's had any place for "the historical Jesus." For Barth what counted was the history of "the Word of God," incarnate in Jesus, discernible in the words of Scripture and in the church's preaching, and encapsulated in the church's long history of attempts to formulate creeds and dogmas. For Bultmann what counted was a direct personal encounter with Jesus, construed as being directly addressed by God, and to which one must respond. This "encounter with Jesus" may sound like the Jesus-piety that was one of the driving forces behind the popular biographies of Jesus—and, indeed, there are strong echoes of Lutheran pietism in Bultmann's theology—but for Bultmann the encounter was a much more austere phenomenon. One met Jesus not in emotional identification with the storied prophet of Nazareth, but purely through the *kerygma*, the "proclamation" about Jesus, which did not announce facts, but demanded decision. The quest for "objective" facts about Jesus was just another of the ways people try to evade the responsibility of that ultimate decision, an example of the "self-contrived security"—like even the sacraments of the church, in Bultmann's hyperprotestant view—that protect us from the austere demand of faith: that we live every moment by fresh decision, unsupported by any structures or certainties. Although in 1926 Bultmann published a book entitled simply *Jesus*, he distanced its intent sharply from that of the *Leben-Jesu* movement, for he was not only convinced "that we can, strictly speaking, know nothing of the personality of Jesus," he thought the whole question was "of secondary importance."[5]

Barth's influence on subsequent investigation of historical questions about Jesus was minimal, and indeed his influence on subsequent New Testament scholarship in general was at best indirect, although the impact of his writings as well as of his strong political and ethical pronouncements during World War II and in the following Cold War was enormous in theological circles in both Europe and the United States. There was one significant exception to the general silence of Barthians on the historical Jesus issue. Hans Frei, who was one of the most important interpreters of Barth in the English-speaking world, took a very special interest, not in the history of Jesus in the modernist sense, but just in the "history-like" narratives of the Gospels, which he took to be the necessary and sufficient representations of "the identity of Jesus Christ"—to be read more in the spirit of the modern realistic novel than in that of historical annals.[6] In later chapters we return to the contribution of Hans Frei and his students to the fundamental questions of interpretation that we have to consider. The path followed by their thinking, however, rarely intersected with the highway on which the juggernaut of the historical Jesus quest rolled forward.

The case of Bultmann and his students was quite different. In the generation after the close of the war, students of Bultmann came to occupy almost every important chair of New Testament studies in German universities. Through the efforts of Americans who studied in Germany, their influence spread also to North America and came to dominate professional debates and much of the scholarly publishing in the field during the fifties, sixties, and seventies. As a result zeal for discovering the historical Jesus flagged, except in those conservative circles that resisted the "thoroughgoing skepticism" (as Schweitzer called it) of the Bultmann school. Ironically, while it had been theological liberals who created the life-of-Jesus movement, undertaking to use the science of history to free Jesus from the dogmas of the later church, now it was conservative theologians—reacting especially to the historical skepticism of the Bultmannians—who undertook to shore up the dogmas by sifting through the Gospels for plausible facts to support the traditional image of Jesus. What was more astonishing was a sudden reappearance of the undead Quest in the heart of the Bultmann camp. In a 1953 meeting of Bultmann's former students, the "Old Marburgers," one of the group's leading lights, Ernst Käsemann, delivered a paper on "The Problem of the Historical Jesus." Käsemann pointed out the ironic "change of fronts" between conservatives and liberals, and urged liberals, at least those of Bultmann's existentialist persuasion, to take seriously again the question of Jesus' earthly identity. Otherwise, the church risked preaching an abstract, "anonymous" gospel, emptying into "moralism and mysticism." That had never been true, he insisted, with the earliest followers of Jesus. However much their memories of Jesus had been shaped by experiences after the crucifixion and the first Easter, those memories still were tied to that earthly individual, in that specific time and place. A biography of Jesus was impossible, Käsemann agreed, but he thought critical exegesis could demonstrate continuity between Jesus' preaching and the preaching of the early Christians.[7]

Bultmann himself remained chary of Käsemann's call for a renewed investigation of the historical Jesus, but others in the camp took up the challenge, and the "New Quest of the Historical Jesus" was born.[8] When I entered graduate school in the early 1960s, the New Quest was in full cry. It has waxed and waned; it has had its successes and failures. By and large, however, the flood of publications by the neoliberal Bultmannians did little to alter the justice of Schweitzer's negative judgment about the Old Quest. The attempt to redefine history in existentialist categories has passed out of fashion, gone the way of the other attempts through the centuries to find what Bultmann called "the right philosophy" by which to translate the myths and mysteries of the New Testament into contemporary thought forms.[9] Once again, however, the modernist longing to discover the true facts about Jesus, to find the hidden key that will explain him with a stroke, proves irrepressible, equally enticing to conservatives and liberals, cultured despisers and naive devotees. Now, several years past retirement, I look back on a half century of this debate, only to find what could well be called a *New* New Quest, churning out books, press releases, and television interviews at a rate ordinarily equaled only by titillating national scandals. My overwhelming sense of déjà vu is perhaps understandable.

There is in fact almost nothing new about the New New quest, as there was little new about the old New Quest. Each of them differs from the old Old Quest of the eighteenth and nineteenth centuries only in one significant respect: we have changed our notions of the ideal Jesus whom we would *like* to find in the sources, and the self-anointed experts obligingly (and profitably) dish up precisely the Jesus who is wanted at the moment. They expertly sift out those disconcerting bits of the tradition that offend (eschatology, final judgment, excessive Jewishness, or whatever), proving by the very latest nineteenth-century techniques that the *real* Jesus could not possibly have said any of those offending things. And they find irrefutable clues in previously unknown documents that Jesus was really just the sort of person we would want writing opinion pieces in our newspapers. The willfulness of the method is surpassed only by the banality of the results.

This is no longer merely a scholar's game, a way of adding some extra income and gaining our fifteen minutes of celebrity. Popular culture has embraced the many Jesuses available for the taking or making, from the sado-masochist Jesus of Mel Gibson to Mary Magdalene's secret lover in the fevered and careless imagination of Dan Brown. Here is the zenith (or the apogee) of the trajectory which began when David Friedrich Strauss constructed "the life of Jesus for the German people," designed for the cheap print culture of the nineteenth century. If it sells one hundred thousand copies or grosses a billion and a half at the box office, it must be true.

Why? What's all the fuss about? Why is the *historical* Jesus, as distinct from just "Jesus," such a big item? As we saw in the previous chapter, that question has its own history. It may be helpful at this point to recapitulate very briefly that history's high points.

"The Flight from Authority"

The history of the historical Jesus is part of what Jeffrey Stout has called "the flight from authority."[10] He depicts the progressive failure of one after the other of those foundations upon which we in the Western world have sought to secure knowledge and trustworthy values since the dawn of the modern age. It is the history of suspicion and disillusionment, but also of constantly renewed hope for freedom in believing and hope in a just social order. It is the story of uncovering the clay feet of public authority, but at the same time the story of a quest for a satisfying private authority—for each of us moderns is torn between our mistrust for the publicly and institutionally certified modes of authority and our longing to be secure in our deepest beliefs and hopes.

Note: this is a distinctly modernist story, one in which we are all characters, whether we think of ourselves as "liberals" or "conservatives." The history of modernism can be written as the tale of *justified suspicions*.

Reformation

The Reformers suspected the papal authorities in Rome. They wanted to be free from institutional control "from across the mountains," and from a penitential system that braced up faith with fear and, incidentally, took a lot of good German *Geld* back to the coffers of St. Peter's. Luther, Calvin, Zwingli, and the rest were by no means individualists in the modern mode, about which I'll have more to say below, but in their emphasis on the personal dimension of sin, on the liberation of conscience, and on the direct clarity of Scripture, they helped to pave the way for that individualism. With their motto *sola scriptura* they dared suggest that every man and woman could read the Bible for himself or herself, and their more complicated doctrine of Scripture's transparency, its *perspicuitas*, implied that the individual reader could make one's own way to the meaning, without help from the clergy, for "popes and councils do err." (The intention of the Reformers was not so simple as that sounds, else they wouldn't have written so many commentaries, but that's another story. We return to this issue in chapter 5.) The point made was this: I can figure out for myself what it all means, so long as no one actively hides the truth from me. And of course, there was usually reason to suspect that people *were* hiding the truth.

Enlightenment

The genie of suspicion, once out of the bottle, is uncontrollable. In the seventeenth and eighteenth centuries groups of intellectuals in London, Edinburgh, Paris, and elsewhere began to suspect not only ecclesiastical hierarchies and structures, but dogmas and traditions of all kinds. Why were we given minds, if not to think things out for ourselves? The great task, the educational task of humankind, was to free the mind, so that the sheer power of reason, once unfettered from external authority, could discover what is indubitably true. When Descartes in his warm stove has doubted all that can reasonably be doubted, there remains that clear and immanent foundation upon which all other knowledge can rest.

Modern Science

The third great movement of doubt, most vivid to us because its aftermath has so transformed the world in our own lifetimes, is the rise of modern science. From the Enlightenment, the pioneers of physics learned to suspect *mystery* and *superstition*. From the deductive science that still prevailed in the Enlightenment, they sought to free the powers of observation and reason, by systematically organizing the process of gathering data, formulating hypotheses, and testing by controlled experiment. Method became the means to truth. Thus by demystifying the world and so liberating ourselves from superstition, now understood as unwarranted belief, we could discover the way the real world works.

A Story of Liberation

I have sketched the story of successive suspicions with perhaps too much academic cynicism. We need to remember that it was always also a story of liberation. It is a story we moderns have lived by, in many variations—a story of progress and of progressive freedom. At its noblest, the story has been a call to arms against our oppressors—even the oppressive superego that resides within ourselves (or did, in any case, in turn-of-the-twentieth-century Vienna). It is a call to set free the individual conscience and the individual's inquiring mind from the oppressive authority of institutions, dogmas, and inherited preju- dices—to see the world as it is, fresh and clean and preg- nant with opportunities for human flourishing.

We are all cynics now. So much of that story's promise rings hollow that we are tempted to reject the whole nar- rative as a delusion. But what then? Do we retreat into new authoritarianisms of our own devising? Or do we fol- low our postmodern hyperawareness into an all-embrac- ing skepticism, into a jaded world in which there is no truth, no transcendence, no lasting thing that is good?

Before we succumb to the opportunism of the right or the cynicism of the left, let us pause to remember the promise. Let us remember that the liberation was some- times real and, when real, always precious. I grew up in the fundamentalist, racist, small-town South, and I rejoice to say that I lived some of that story of liberation. I am pro- foundly grateful for what Reformation, Enlightenment, and Science have done for me, and I'm not about to throw that away.

The Negatives

Nevertheless it is true that the story of liberation leaves out some important things. And the modernist strug- gles—both on the part of the proponents of modernism and of its reactionary opponents—have led into blind alleys in theology and biblical interpretation. Those blind alleys constrict and distort the perennial "quest of the historical Jesus." Four aspects of modern theology and biblical interpretation seem to me at fault here:

1. The modernist/fundamentalist controversies a century ago have left us with a habit of privileging literalism on both sides of a polarized debate. The mistake came, as Hans Frei has so carefully explained, in supposing that, if we say that the Bible is true, we must mean that it *refers* accurately to facts of nature or to historical events. Other ways in which a narrative might *mean* and might convey truth were systematically "eclipsed."[11] Note that both sides of the controversies were caught in this same trap. On the one side were the historical critics, who triumphantly demonstrated that it wasn't likely that Jesus *really* said this or that, or that several of the stories about him seemed to presuppose a situation like that of the early church rather than the context of Jesus' own time in Roman Galilee and Judaea, and so on. On the other side were the true believers, using the same positivistic methods of archaeology and historiography to show that, yes, everything did happen just as the Bible says. So in the modernist era, what had been called "the plain sense of the text" or "the literal meaning" came to signify something quite different from what those phrases had meant in the premodern eras. We return to this question in a later chapter.

2. The second distortion of our way of questioning has been an unconscious acceptance of what George Lindbeck has called a cognitivist model of religion.[12] We have been seduced by a long history of theological debates to think that beliefs and doctrines define faith—both for believers and for antibelievers. That is only natural, considering that the debates have been carried on by people

who earn their living as professional theologians in theological seminaries and faculties. However, the cognitivist model of religion also trickled down to laypeople, distorting not only their understanding of who they were, but also their way of asking the question who Jesus was. Among Roman Catholics, the cognitivist model was transmitted to ordinary believers largely through catechetical practice—"the Baltimore Catechism" shaped the understanding of many a Catholic of earlier generations—but always within a liturgical and communal context that prevented the isolation of doctrine alone in the formation of the Christian life. It can be argued that doctrine became much more determinative of Protestant self-understanding, as an inheritance from the post-Reformation conflicts both between Protestants and Catholics and among the multiplying Protestant sects. Especially the Fundamentalist movement in the United States, beginning immediately after World War I, persuaded many laypeople that their standing within or without the faith depended on their affirmation or denial of a discrete list of particular, controverted propositions—like the Virgin Birth of Jesus or the "inerrancy" of Scripture. Such formulas are really shibboleths of controversy, not rules of life. A moment's reflection is enough to show most of us that no short list of propositions can describe the center of faith. Theology is the grammar of the faithful life, in one helpful formulation, but language is more than grammar, and life more than both.

3. The third distortion is the pervasive individualism of the modern Western world. In the religious realm this individualism is expressed in the nostrum that we hear every day, repeated as if it were as self-evident as sunrise: "religion is a private matter." We should recognize that this formulation expresses primarily a political policy,

enshrined in the Bill of Rights of the U.S. Constitution, that the governing authorities are not to determine religious belief or practice. That was a lesson which the founding fathers of the nation had learned from the bitter experience of the religious wars of premodern Europe— and perhaps from the religious establishments in several of the American colonies. This legal policy has been rather successful, on the whole, in the American experience, but when shorthand formulations of it are mistaken for a description of the way religion works, the result is utter confusion. We have seen many examples of that confusion in recent years, some deliberately fostered by political factions that have wanted to breach the constitutional wall between church and state. It is important, accordingly, that we think carefully about the social realities of individual identity, not least for the sake of those political liberties that have too often been argued on the basis of a naive individualism. In fact, religion, for good or ill, has always been anything but a private matter, and we do not begin to understand religious phenomena if we ignore their social and communal dimensions.

4. The fourth distortion of modern religion is romanticism. Though theologians operate with a cognitivist model, as if concepts were life, for most of us feeling ultimately trumps rationality. And when we talk about who we really are, self-consciousness and self-awareness are central to the way we think about our identity.

Literalism, cognitivism, privatism, and romanticism all affect our sense of who we are—of what it means to be a particular person. And they all necessarily affect the way we think about the identity of Jesus, for every age uses its own taken-for-granted models of identity when it tries to describe the person of Jesus. Those good old hymns we loved to sing at summer camp are very revealing. "What a Friend We Have in Jesus!" "Jesus, Lover of My Soul!" "Jesus, the very thought of Thee/ With sweetness fills the breast;/ But sweeter far Thy face to see,/ And in thy presence rest." "Jesus loves me, this I know, for the Bible tells me so." And of course, that tryst in the garden, all alone, when the dew is still on the roses:

> And He walks with me, and He talks with me,
> And He tells me I am His own;
> And the joy we share as we tarry there,
> None other has ever known.

Now it would be unfair to suggest that this kind of romanticism, even eroticism, is only a modern phenomenon—one of the verses quoted here was written by Bernard of Clairvaux, after all. But the ubiquity of the first-person singular in these verses, the sentimentality, the absence of any concern for the world beyond the two lovers—all these are the signs of modern romantic religion, the kind of Christianity that insists that the only question that counts is, "Do you take Jesus as your *personal savior*?"

Even Albert Schweitzer, after brilliantly cataloguing the excesses and failures of the "Life of Jesus Movement," turns back at the end of the book to a lonely romanticism: Jesus, freed from the shackles of ecclesiastical doctrine, "comes to us as One unknown, without a name, as of old, by the lakeside, he came to those men who did not know who he was. He says the same words: 'Follow me!'"[13] Schweitzer writes his own romantic biography of Jesus, and then he goes off to meet the mysterious stranger in the jungles of Lambarene.

In the long history of Christianity there have been quite

other ways of thinking about who Jesus is. Put alongside those romantic hymns around the campfire this, the very earliest hymn we know from the followers of Jesus:

> [Hymn] the anointed Jesus,
> who had the very shape of God
> but did not count it windfall
> to be God's equal,
> but emptied himself,
> taking shape of slave:
> becoming of human likeness
> and found in human guise,
> he humbled himself—
> obedient to point of death:
> yes, of the cross's death.
>
> Therefore God has raised him high,
> conferred on him the name
> that's higher than every name,
> so at the name of Jesus
> every knee must bend:
> heavenly and earthly and infernal all,
> and every tongue must loudly own
> the Lord is Jesus Christ,
> to the glory of Father God.[14]

That doesn't sound very much like your typical "Mediterranean peasant," nor your average "marginal Jew." Leaving aside for the moment the question of the accuracy of those modern portraits, the Jesus they depict was not the one who made history. It was not the Mediterranean peasant nor the marginalized folk hero nor the supposed Galilean Cynic who produced the vast swerve in cultural history that we know as Christianity. It was the mysterious god-equal figure of the hymn, whose crucifixion was not merely one more slaughter in the routine of colonial brutality, was more than mere martyrdom, was beyond the pathos of crushed innocence—of all of which his time, like ours, had seen far too many examples. In the poetry of the early Christians, that shameful death became the pivot of the human story, the supreme model of grace, God's ultimate self-revelation. It is, of course, difficult for academic historians to believe that poetry can make history—but that, I submit, is what happened.

But what is the process that yielded that poetry? That is, I think, one of the most interesting of the questions that have teased modern biblical scholarship. How did that Galilean carpenter become the god-equal envoy from heaven, the last Adam, the new *anthrōpos*, God's partner in creation, the savior of the world, the Son of God, the Lord of heaven and earth and hell? It is not for want of trying by generations of learned and ingenious scholars that our understanding of the process remains unsatisfying. Neither is the problem entirely the result of scarce and fragmentary evidence. Rather, the whole modernist project suffers from several serious flaws, which have skewed our perception of the questions we need to be asking about Christianity's origins. All follow from those four basic distortions that I described above, the fallacies of literalism, cognitivism, individualism, and romanticism. One of the resultant flaws in our reading of the past is the Eureka Complex—our natural tendency, upon the discovery of some new and exciting bit of evidence from the past, to seize upon it as a key to open all doors. Another is the habit of treating broad cultural abstractions as if they were real *things* that could cause other things to happen. A third is a romantic conception of personal identity.

The Romance of Novelty

In the 1750s treasure hunters dug into the ruins of ancient Herculaneum, a rich suburb of Naples that had been buried, along with nearby Pompeii, by the eruption of Vesuvius in 79 CE. In one of the villas they found a large number of rolls of inscribed papyrus, the ancient paper made in Egypt for several millennia from the pith of marsh reeds. Although all the rolls were charred, and many would not be successfully opened and read until the twentieth century, these documents from antiquity immediately caused great excitement. Many of them were works of the famous teacher of Epicurean philosophy, mentioned by Cicero and others, Philodemus of Gadara, who had taught at Herculaneum and Naples. The thought that such a chance discovery could suddenly provide a window into the life and thought of the past—could bring back to life the thinking of a person who had hitherto been only a name in the record—revived that zeal for recovering the sources of Western culture that had inspired the Renaissance four centuries earlier. Soon travelers from Egypt began to bring back more bits of papyri, unearthed from the dry sands of that country; the first was presented to Cardinal Stefano Borgia in 1778. A century later, systematic excavations began in several places. Those excavations and further chance finds eventually produced thousands of pages. Among them were not only literary works, including many copies of early Christian writings both known and previously unknown, but also official and private letters, contracts, wills, commercial documents, and all kinds of bits and pieces representing the transactions of everyday life.[15]

As the documents on papyri began to be published in ever larger numbers, scholars of ancient Christianity slowly came to see that they could have revolutionary implications for our understanding of Christian beginnings, in three areas. Most obvious was the discovery of copies of portions of the New Testament itself that were earlier than any manuscript previously known. In a few instances, they had been made within a century of the composition of the document. As this papyrological evidence was assimilated, the science of textual criticism was transformed.[16] New critical editions of the Greek New Testament began to appear with accelerating regularity, and new translations taking advantage of them followed swiftly—sometimes to the consternation of pious readers who found some of their favorite passages changed or even relegated to footnotes when they turned out to be missing from the oldest and most reliable manuscripts.[17]

The second area of biblical studies on which the papyri shone new light was the character of the Greek language in which the books of New Testament, as well as the Greek translation of the Hebrew Scriptures, which had been the Bible of most of the first Christians, were written. The Greek in which all modern readers of the Bible had been trained was based on classical Greek literature, mostly from the fifth and fourth centuries BCE. The differences between classical style and that of the New Testament were palpable. In antiquity, well-educated converts sometimes apologized for the crude style of the Gospels, suggesting that it represented the condescension of the Holy Spirit to the capacity of ordinary folk. In modern times, however, a more ingenious suggestion had carried the day: the New Testament writers used a new dialect of Greek, a unique, sacred language, a "Holy Ghost language." A slightly less overtly pious version of this conceit was the suggestion that the Greek of the New Testament (like that of the Septuagint) was largely controlled by Hebrew and

Aramaic idiom.[18] Both these notions were to be shattered when a young pastor and lecturer in theology, Adolf Deissmann, happened on a publication of some of the new papyri. At once he saw that the language of the New Testament was very like the language of the private letters, legal documents, handbooks, and other miscellany of everyday life found in the nonliterary papyri. Many of the very words of the New Testament that had puzzled philologians turned up in the papyri—and in the inscriptions in stone that were also being collected and published in ever greater numbers and with ever greater skill. Far from being a unique dialect, a "Holy Ghost language," the language of the first Christian writers was the "common" language, the *koinē* of ordinary people.[19]

Deissmann also saw that the new evidence could not only expand our understanding of the words and grammar of the New Testament, it could also give fresh insights into the social and cultural environment to which the first Christians belonged. He observed that "by its social structure primitive Christianity points unequivocally to the lower and middle classes. . . . Until recently these masses were almost entirely lost to the historian. Now however, thanks to the discovery of their own authentic records, they have suddenly risen again from the rubbish mounds of the ancient cities, little market towns, and villages."[20]

The fresh ideas introduced into historical thinking about the first Christians by evidence from the papyri and inscriptions were almost entirely salutary in their effects. Yet these insights were not immune from the distortions of the Eureka Complex. For example, among the most fascinating of the papyri were many that contained exact prescriptions for obtaining desired ends by magical means—harming an enemy, winning a lover, curing a disease. These spells and recipes offered new insight into popular beliefs and practices in antiquity (not to mention the demimonde of later ages). In that context the stories of Jesus' miracles took on quite a different dimension. The resulting questions about the way those stories would have been heard by people in the first century were altogether different from the questions raised about miracles by the seventeenth- and eighteenth-century rationalists, with their division of the world between "natural" and "supernatural," or the nineteenth-century positivists, with their disdain of "superstition" in their scientifically "disenchanted" world. Inevitably, however, these new insights were subject to exaggeration—so that sometimes "Jesus the magician" was made to seem the *only* or at least the *determining* image that contemporaries of Jesus would have formed of him.[21]

The other insights gleaned from the papyri were also subject to one-sidedness in application, and they could even tempt the scholars most intensely involved with them to the myopia or hubris of imagining that they had discovered the interpretive key to unlock the secret of Christian beginnings. Deissmann's healthy observations about the popular quality of much of the Greek in the New Testament, for example, tempted some to see earliest Christianity as a "proletarian" movement and thus to "explain" the phenomenon as the product of class conflict.[22] Even the advances in linguistics and textual criticism were not immune to such temptations, in this case the temptation to imagine that we could now reconstruct the *original* text and, moreover, with our improved knowledge of the ancient context and ancient language usage, the *original meaning* of the text. These turned out to be dangerous illusions.[23]

The papyri are only one example of discoveries that have contributed to our knowledge and understanding of antiquity and, as a result, to the contexts in which Jesus and his followers were at home, thus sparking imaginative new ways of asking after their identity—yet, inevitably it seems, also tempting scholars to "magic key" reductionism in our writing of history. We have only to recall the enormous—and justified—excitement generated by the discovery of the Dead Sea Scrolls in the caves of Wadi Qumran beginning in 1947 and sustained by subsequent discoveries and by the long, tedious process of reassembling fragments, publishing, and translating them. As we shall see in the next chapter, these texts not only led to important revisions in our understanding of the varieties of ancient Judaism, they also provided parallels to some aspects of the early sect of Jesus' followers that, by careful comparisons, have illuminated some of our fundamental questions about the Jesus group's ways of interpreting both Scripture and their world. However, the discoveries brought—and even now continue to evoke occasionally— sensationalist claims about their relation to Jesus and Christianity. One of the earliest scholars to examine them carefully jumped to the conclusion that the mysterious "Teacher of Righteousness" mentioned but never named in the scrolls was a precursor in almost every way to Jesus—"Prophet, Man of Sorrows and Head of the Church."[24] Much of the evidence for those claims turned out to be in editorial reconstructions of what *might* have been contained in the numerous holes and missing pages, but that did not diminish the *frisson* of scandal. Other proposals were more far-fetched: the Teacher of Righteousness, one writer insists, was in fact John the Baptist, and his enemy "the wicked Priest" was none other than Jesus.[25] And so on. The long delays in publication, which seemed inexplicable to outsiders who had never actually experienced the tedium of piecing together odd fragments of leather that had broken apart and molded under many centuries' accumulation of bat guano in caves, contributed to conspiracy theories: surely some secret group in the Vatican (were not some of the leading scholars priests?) was suppressing some dark secret about Jesus.[26]

Equally sensational and even longer coming fully into the public eye were the leather-bound papyrus codices (that is, bound like modern books rather than scrolls) found near the Upper Egyptian village Nag Hammadi in 1945, and commonly called "The Nag Hammadi Gnostic Library" (although only some of the documents are "Gnostic" in any strict sense, and there is no convincing evidence that the collection comprised "a library"). The importance of these documents in expanding our pictures of the variety and creativity of the Christian movement between the second and the fourth centuries is hard to exaggerate. Now we have not only the church fathers' disdainful descriptions of those sectarians who called themselves "the Knowing Ones," the *gnōstikoi* or "Gnostics," and related or parallel movements, but through the new discoveries we have long-lost documents from those groups themselves—and from other, less easily identified groups who were also eventually forced to the sidelines in the competition of ideas and practice that by and by produced the Catholic or Orthodox tradition. Among them are new Gospels, some of them previously known by name from references by the antiheretical writers of the church but none of them seen by anyone for many centuries—the Gospel of Truth, perhaps written by the famous archheretic Valentinus himself; the Gospel according to Philip; the Gospel according to Thomas; the Gospel of the Egyptians. These Gospels, set alongside the canonical four, raised altogether new questions about the different ways in which Christians in the early centuries constructed the identity of Jesus, their own identity, and their understanding of their world. Here was a Jesus, for example, who could say things like, "Split a piece of wood: I am there. Lift a stone, and you (plur.) will find me there" (Jesus incarnate as centipede?). Or "See, I am going to attract her [Mary] to make her male so that she too might become a living spirit that resembles you males. For every woman who makes herself male will enter the kingdom of heaven." Or this particularly tantalizing saying, unfortunately fragmentary, "The wisdom who is called barren wisdom is the mother [of the] angels. And the companion of the [...] Mary Magdalene. The [......] loved her more than [all] the disciples, [and he used to] kiss her on her [... more] often than the rest of the [disciples] [...]. They said to him, 'Why do you love her more than all of us?' The savior answered, saying to them, 'Why do I not love you like her?'"[27] Ample material to fire the imagination of historian and novelist alike.

There were more general discoveries as well that changed our understanding of the past. Cumulatively, the evolving technology of archaeology uncovered not merely the awe-inspiring remains of great cities from Ephesus to Petra, from Bath to Carthage, but more and more insights into the way in which people lived their daily lives, managed their diets, organized their relationships, remembered their dead. The implications for understanding how the new subculture of the Christians emerged within that environment can hardly be overestimated. Yet until fairly recently those implications were ignored in much of "biblical archaeology" in favor of attempts to prove or disprove details of the biblical narrative by finding physical evidence of, say, the fall of Jericho or the house of Peter in Capernaum. Once again, scientific method was succumbing to that modernist literalism of both left and right mentioned above. Sometimes the results were ludicrous. When one scholar reported that he had found an extinct volcano that was no doubt the "mountain . . . burning with fire" of Deuteronomy 5:23 (NRSV), another scholar asked sarcastically if he had also found the mountains that "skipped like rams" (Ps. 114:4, NRSV). Sensitivity to metaphor has not always been a hallmark of modernist inquiry.

Discoveries that changed our constructions of history were not always the result of digging literally in the earth; often they came from patient digging through artifacts and documents stored uncatalogued in libraries or museum basements, or by the meticulous labor of philologians to translate languages little known in the West and thus to bring to the attention of Western historians documents used by groups and sects and ethnic communities little studied by modern scholars. Such, for example, were the sacred writings of an obscure baptizing sect still living on the border of modern Iraq and Iran, known by some as "the Mandaeans." When these began to be translated into German by the Semitic philologian Marc Lidzbarski, several New Testament scholars noted at once an uncanny resemblance of some of their poetic sections to portions of the Gospel of John. Rudolf Bultmann seized upon this resemblance to propose an elaborate reconstruction of the prehistory of that Gospel. Because the Mandaeans (whose name in Aramaic meant "the Knowing Ones," and so seemed the equivalent of "Gnostics") also had stories of John the Baptist and, indeed, a Book of John among their scriptures, it must be, Bultmann reasoned, that they began as that very sect of John the Baptist to whom Jesus himself had once belonged and from which the followers of Jesus, when they broke away to follow Jesus as the Messiah, had to distinguish themselves. Some one of those

Baptists, Bultmann suggested, had converted to the Jesus sect, bringing with him some of that special poetry, originally about John the Baptist, pictured as a divine messenger who had come down from heaven to save those elect who were able to become Gnostics. The converted Baptist used that myth and rewrote those poems to describe Jesus, and so constructed the first version of the Gospel of John. Backed by sharp exegetical insights and meticulously detailed and ingenious stylistic analysis, Bultmann's hypothesis was one of the most brilliant constructions of twentieth-century New Testament scholarship. Unfortunately, further investigation of the Mandaeans showed that it could not stand, while Bultmann's rather willful reconstruction of the sources supposedly used by the Fourth Evangelist and of the complex history of subsequent revision of the Gospel ultimately proved unconvincing to most scholars as well.[28]

In the nineteenth century, the edition, publication, and translation of obscure documents had already brought to the attention of New Testament specialists a number of pieces of literature of Jewish origin which lay outside the rabbinic canon of Scripture, but which in some places showed certain resonances with the imagery and ideas of early Christianity. Many of these texts came to be collected under the artificial and ultimately misleading title, "the Pseudepigrapha ['false writings,' usually applied to writings under an assumed name] of the Old Testament."[29] Among those that attracted the most interest early on were some that seemed generically very like the New Testament Revelation of John as well as the book of Daniel and certain chapters in the prophetic books of the Old Testament. From the word John used to describe his book, *apocalypsis*, "unveiling" or "revelation" (Rev. 1:1), these all came to be called "apocalypses," and much scholarly labor has been

invested ever since in defining just what characteristics are
necessary and sufficient for a book to be so labeled.[30] Even
more urgent and more difficult were the questions: Who
used books like this? Why did so many writings in this
form apparently become popular right around the time
that Jesus appeared? Soon some investigators began to
speculate that these writings represented some ancient,
deviant movement within Judaism, characterized by
expectation of an immediate end to world history and a
transformation of the world by God's intervention to
introduce a new age of righteousness, heralded by visionaries who (through the visions recounted in these apocalypses) foresaw the events that would bring in that new age.
The movement, or its ideal type, was dubbed in German
die Apokalyptik and in English "apocalypticism." To many
it seemed that it must have been precisely out of the
atmosphere and the hopes of apocalypticism that Jesus
and his disciples emerged, and that it was "apocalyptic
eschatology" that was the key to explain Jesus' fundamental teachings and actions. Jesus' talk about "the kingdom
of God," in that case, had little or nothing to do with that
progressive improvement of social relationships that late-
nineteenth-century liberal Protestants had understood by
the term, but was precisely an apocalyptic category: not a
kingdom that humans could bring about, but a transformation of the world order that only God's miraculous
intervention through his chosen messenger, his Messiah,
could accomplish. The liberal scholar Johannes Weiss
summed up this conclusion in his little book, "Jesus'
Preaching of the Kingdom of God," which fell like a
bombshell among the Protestant liberals of turn-of-the-
century Germany. We have already seen how Albert
Schweitzer popularized Weiss's "consistent eschatology"
and wrote his own biography of Jesus, based on the con-

viction that Jesus must have understood himself as that eschatological messenger of the new age, and thus died disillusioned when God failed to act as expected.[31] As we have seen, the discovery of the Dead Sea Scrolls gave new life to these speculations, but ultimately required a radical revision of the assumptions of earlier scholarship. "Apocalypticism," however, continues to hold sway as one of those master keys that is supposed to explain the birth of Christianity. It is a construct that has taught us many things, but it is a modern construct. No one in first-century Palestine would have said, "I am an apocalypticist," or would have known what we were talking about if we could ask if he believed in "apocalypticism."

Confusing Names with Causes

Apocalypticism is one of those modern constructions which serve the very useful purposes of organizing large quantities of data and comparing different bodies of information sharing some family resemblance, but which may tempt us into a dangerous shortcut in our thinking. Once we have grown accustomed to using the term, it is very easy to slip into the assumption that "apocalypticism" was a real entity, something that could cause other things to happen. Why, we ask, did the people of the Dead Sea Scrolls withdraw into their isolated settlement in the desert? And we answer, because they were an apocalyptic movement. Why did Jesus talk about the kingdom of God? Because he was an apocalyptic prophet. And so on. Such abbreviated statements may do no harm so long as we remember that they are shorthand ways of referring to very much more complicated situations, but all too often they fool us into imagining that we have *explained* phenomena when we have only named or classified them.

"Apocalypticism" is only one of the many scholarly constructs that have tempted us to confuse names with explanations. "Gnosticism" was another that played an immense but often ill-defined rôle in twentieth-century explanations of parts of the New Testament and later developments in early Christian history. Perhaps the most pervasive of all such models is the conceit that the evolution of Christianity can be explained at its core as part of a great struggle, dominating the whole Mediterranean world from the time of Alexander the Great to the dawn of the Byzantine Christian empire, between two cultures: "Judaism" and "Hellenism." Sometimes the categories were even broader: "Orientalism" versus "Western civilization," but the "Judaism versus Hellenism" model was the one that came to dominate reconstructions of early Christian history. This scheme first entered the arsenal of biblical historians through the proposals of Ferdinand Christian Baur, a professor of Protestant theology at the University of Tübingen. Baur was trying to make sense of the conflict described in Acts 6 between "the Hellenists" and "the Hebrews" among Christians in Jerusalem. Taking further clues from the speech of Stephen in Acts 7, identified as a leader of the Hellenists, and from the repeated conflicts addressed by Paul in his letters, and remembering the then-standard reading of the Maccabee rebellion against Antiochus IV Epiphanes, Baur undertook to solve with one stroke multiple puzzles about Christian beginnings. The conflict in Jerusalem was not just a squabble over money, but was rather one of fundamental theology. On the one side was the original "Jewish-Christian" community led by Jesus' immediate apostles and by his brother James. On the other were "Hellenized" Jews who had a vision of a universal religion breaking through the boundaries of

Judaism in a mission to Gentiles. Of the latter group the apostle Paul, after his conversion, was destined to be the leader. And the conflict between them, which Baur saw mirrored in Paul's chief letters, especially Galatians and 2 Corinthians, determined the development of the new religion. Baur made his discoveries just as Hegel's philosophy was becoming the rage in theological circles; it was easy for him to see "Judaism" or "Jewish Christianity" as the thesis that provoked among Jesus' more enlightened followers, and especially and uniquely the apostle Paul, the antithesis "Gentile Christianity." Efforts to resolve the conflict would eventually produce, as the synthesis, "early Catholicism."[32]

The ingenuity of the scheme is apparent. It is also obvious that "Judaism" and "Hellenism" here are code words for complex sets of ideas masquerading as historical entities. On the one side is the particularity of a national or ethnic religion; on the other, the universal religion for all humankind. On the one hand, the limited and conditioned facts of historical circumstance; on the other, the universal truths of reason. On the one hand, flesh; on the other, spirit. On the one hand, "legalism"; on the other, freedom. As Baur in one place could put it quite bluntly, "Judaism is nothing more than the religion of the law in contradistinction to Christianity, which is the religion of the spirit."[33]

Baur was not alone in seeing cultural conflict, and specifically the conflict between Judaism and Hellenism, as the secret engine that drove the whole process that would produce Christendom. It was J. G. Droysen, a younger contemporary of Baur, who adopted the term *Hellenismus* for what he described as the beginning point of "the history of history," the epoch of Alexander and his "Successors." Informed by the use of the Greek word in

2 Maccabees 4:13 and, like Baur, by the report of the dispute of the "Hellenists" in Acts 6:1, and also, again like Baur, indebted to Hegel's dialectical theory of history, Droysen saw in the confrontation between Judaism and paganism in the Hellenistic world "the last and deepest opposition." That opposition—not only between "Western" and "Oriental" civilizations, but also between the solidarity of human experience inscribed in tradition and the liberating but corrosive powers of reason—must be reconciled if the "history of human freedom" were ever to come to fruition. That reconciliation, Droysen asserted, was the task given by history to Christianity.[34]

The battleground metaphors of the Judaism-versus-Hellenism model have been very fruitful in historical research for more than a century and a half, and the model still persists in much current scholarship. Yet the underlying oversimplifications that made it possible have again and again blinded us to facts that did not fit it. Gradually the accumulation of such facts, driven in part by new discoveries and new ways of analyzing data, has made the model untenable. No longer, for example, is it possible, as it was only a generation or two ago, to imagine that the development from the teachings of Jesus to the exalted figure of the Christ found, for example, in that hymn quoted in Philippians 2 which we discussed above, is a move from "Palestinian Judaism" through "Hellenistic diaspora Judaism" to "pagan Hellenism."[35] The picture today looks much less simple.

Christianity begins its existence as one among several competing Jewish sects or movements. Judaism was not one thing, either in Judaea and Galilee or in the Diaspora. Nor were the boundaries among the varieties of Judaism fixed or impermeable. Not surprisingly, then, we see variety also in early Christian groups, from the earliest moment we can detect their character in our sources. The adjectives "Jewish" and "Hellenistic" are practically no help at all in sorting out that variety.

Like the other varieties of Judaism, the earliest Christian groups are simultaneously Jewish and Hellenistic. The questions that have to be asked are more particular: Which parts of the Jewish tradition are being assumed and reinterpreted by this or that group of early Christians? Which institutions are continued, which discarded? From the side of the larger society, what signs are there in a given Christian document that the author is employing a commonplace from the philosophical schools or a verbal strategy taught in the rhetorical schools? Or would a certain turn of phrase remind the hearers of notions that we can learn at second hand from the magical spells and handbooks that have turned up in such abundance? Again and again we find that the more broadly we cast our nets, the more interpretive fish we bring up. Most people in antiquity, we must surmise, did not know that they were supposed to stay firmly in one or another of our ideal types.[36]

Another Model of Identity

One fatal flaw in the modernist project of Jesus research is the romantic model of personal identity that has controlled our post-Enlightenment construction of the self. Each of us imagines that the real *I* is a unique, mysterious entity, utterly individual and never fully knowable by anyone else. The self is identified with my consciousness of self, which may of course be deceived, but which is mine, mine alone. The introspective, radically individual conception of personal identity receives its apotheosis in Freud's topography of the self. The mysterious consciousness,

buried deep within each person by the process of social-
ization, stands over against an antagonistic social world
that has, beginning with its birth, distorted, restricted, and
obscured it. The public persona, the identity that others
see, hides and may obliterate, even from our own awareness, the real "I."

In an intellectual world dominated by the introspective
conception of the self, it is easy to see why the "quest of
the historical Jesus" has so often taken the form of a search
to discover Jesus' "self-consciousness." That was the
watchword in British and American scholarship of the first
half of the twentieth century: "Jesus' messianic self-consciousness." The ultimate question was, "Who did Jesus
understand himself to be?" Conservative as well as liberal
scholars labored to show that Jesus did think of himself as
the Messiah and of God as his father, and that therefore
there was an unbroken continuity between that self-
awareness and what the early church said about him.
Many continental scholars, on the other hand, tended to
be more skeptical, positing a sharp divide between the
"Jesus of history" and "the church's Christ"; between
Jesus' own sense of self and mission and the creative constructions of the early communities that were shaped by
their belief in Jesus' resurrection. Oftentimes the question
is put in rather simplistic terms: Did Jesus think he was the
Messiah, or not—as if "the Messiah" had been a fixed and
well-known concept that Jesus could just slip into, like a
suit of clothes. That misleading simplification is one of
many that have been demolished by discoveries of recent
decades, to which I return a bit later. But even more
sophisticated ways of putting the question have, all too
often, assumed without question the romantic, individualistic construction of personal identity.

There is, however, quite a different way of thinking about personal identity, which is prevalent in the social sciences and in some forms of present-day literary theory. It begins by asking the simple question, "How did I come to know who I am?—How did I become a conscious self?" And instead of imagining some transcendent substance in me, this way of inquiry remembers how a baby begins to respond to the mother's smiles; how baby-talk is met by answering parent-talk; how touch and warmth transmit affection and caring and limits; how, as language skills grow, the world of the "significant others" expands and my story begins to interact with the stories of all who speak to me and, potentially, of all who have written and spoken in my language community.

Many thinkers in several different fields have come to see self-identity in this way. To name only one of them, Mikhail Bakhtin, the Russian literary critic, constructs a dialogic model of the self. One becomes a person not in opposition to society, but precisely through society—and through language, the primary instance of sociality. "Any instance of self-awareness . . . is an act of gauging oneself against some social norm. . . . In becoming aware of myself, I attempt to look at myself, as it were, through the eyes of another person."[37] Bakhtin was following the Russian psychologist Lev Vygotsky, who rejected Freud's opposition between self and society. "In Freud, self is suppressed in the service of the social; in Bakhtin, self is precisely a function of the social. In Freud, the more of the other, the less of the self; in Bakhtin, the more of the other, the more of the self."[38] Coincidentally, this dialogic model of the self sounds very much like the earlier American psychologist George Herbert Mead, who emphasized the role of the "significant other" in the making of the self.[39]

Selfhood is a process. It grows through an endless series of transactions with other persons, within a specific social and cultural complex. It flourishes through language, which makes the dialogue possible. This social-transactionist conception of the self has in fact become quite widely shared by psychologists in the field of social cognition—ironically, as much from their reading of Bakhtin as from rediscovering Mead.[40]

Would it not make sense to use the dialectical, social model of the self in our inquiries into the identity of history-forming personages of the past? In the case of Jesus, this would mean that we would no longer drive a wedge between the "real" inner Jesus, known only to himself and (it is claimed) a few modern scholars, and the images of Jesus formed by his followers. The complicating factor, of course, is that the notion of the "significant other" would now have to be extended beyond the formative years of the subject—indeed, beyond the (earthly) lifetime of the subject, for the social transactions that produced the Jesus we are able to know happened for the most part after his death. Nevertheless, it seems to me that such a move offers a more realistic picture of the Jesus of history, that is, the Jesus who has made history. What we have to describe is not some hidden, inner core of what Jesus knew himself to be, with all socially constructed layers of the self peeled away, but precisely the dialogical process by which those early followers of Jesus constructed their own identity at the very same time they were constructing Jesus' identity. It may sound overly bold to say that Jesus *is* the persona he becomes in interaction with others. I defer to systematic theologians to say what the Trinitarian implications might be, though I think to propose a christology in terms of such a process may not be quite so heretical as it sounds.

Implications

We should have learned by now that there are no final answers in the writing of history. Every age has its own blind spots, its own unconscious preconceptions, its prejudices; every age also has its fresh discoveries, its new ways of asking questions, and new voices in the debate about what happened in the past. All this is abundantly illustrated by the history of the quest for the so-called historical Jesus. In this essay I am not proposing the ultimate way of understanding who Jesus was. I am not going to reveal the secret Jesus, long concealed by this or that conspiratorial agency or the loss of *the* magic manuscript. (Although I might reconsider, if someone offers me a large enough advance on the movie rights.) I am proposing that, when we ask after Jesus' *persona*, we allow ourselves to ask the kinds of questions we would ask about ourselves, or about other persons in the present or in the past, that is, to adopt a social, transactional model of the self. This will not yield the *ultimate* picture of Jesus, the *real* Jesus. But it may help us to escape that romantic, introspective, individualistic, privatist model of identity that has shaped too much of the modernist Quest.

The model of selfhood I am suggesting takes identity to be a process, not a substance—a process, lifelong, not a once-for-all, unchanging thing that is oneself. To say that Jesus, like the rest of us, becomes who he is may sound shocking—but that is the original scandal of the incarnation as it was heard by the sophisticated Middle Platonists of antiquity: that God should involve Godself in becoming. And my proposal is the modern counterpart to the ancient learned doctrine that responded to the scandal, the Enhypostatic Union. It is another way of saying that Jesus becomes a human person as we all do: by interaction with the others around him. All those questions asked by other characters in the Gospel stories—"Who is this, that even the winds and waves obey him?" "Is this not Joseph's son?" "Where did this man get all this? . . . Is not this the carpenter, the son of Mary and brother of James and Joses and Judas and Simon, and are not his sisters here with us?" "Who *is* this 'Son of the Human'?" "Are you the King of the Jews?" "Are you the One Who is Coming, or must we expect another?"—those questions are not clues in a game of Twenty Questions. The answer is not there all along to be guessed; the answer is in the making, and the Evangelists have each written their different stories in such a way that *we* the readers must involve ourselves in the process. The identity of Jesus, like all human identity, is a process, not a given. The identity of Jesus, like all human identity, is social, not only introspective and private.

We only become human persons through language: that is the primary and definitive medium of our transactions with the significant others with and through whom we become who we are. In the words of Hannah Arendt, "from the time of our birth we are immersed in 'a web of narratives,' of which we are both the author and the object."[41] We become who we are through the stories others tell of us and the stories we tell of ourselves.

That insight provides us with one further clue for our asking who Jesus is: the process of identity formation is an interpretive process. In every culture there are some master narratives that describe the way life is, and there are some typical characters in those narratives. Every individual has to find her or his story within that master narrative, and all the significant others around that person are also engaged in telling and retelling those stories and thus in the continual process of interpretation. The next chapter examines a few of the ways in which people in the environment of Jesus interpreted life in their place and time. With those interpretive strategies as context, we look at some examples of the ways the earliest followers of Jesus engaged with their memories of him in a very complicated process of interpretation. In this case it was a process that not only made places for him within several of the master narratives of that culture, but which in the long run changed those narratives forever and in that way made history.

Chapter Three

Memory and Invention
The Making of Jesus Christ

The characters who encounter Jesus in the Gospel narratives are full of questions: "Who is this, that even the winds and waves obey him?" "Is this not Joseph's son?" "Where did this man get all this? . . . Is not this the carpenter, the son of Mary and brother of James and Joses and Judas and Simon, and are not his sisters here with us?" "Who *is* this 'Son of the Human'?" "Are you the One Who is Coming, or must we expect another?" "Are you the King of the Jews?" I suggested in the previous chapter that such questions represent that process of interpersonal transactions by which identity is made. Here we see the intersection of narratives, the trying on of roles, the groping for understanding by which the social, dialogical self comes into being. The questions are embedded in stories shaped by both tradition and authoring, stories written to be declaimed, performed in communities for which they mattered supremely. The characters are entryways into those stories for those engaged hearers of the gospel. The characters are the hearers' surrogates for their own questioning. And those questioners, the ones in the stories and the ones listening to the stories, in asking who Jesus is, are at the same time placing themselves in the intersecting narratives, and so implicitly asking who *they* are. By writing those stories down, the evangelists have put us as readers into that position, too. Asking after the identity of Jesus is a self-involving process, as the varied narratives about him intersect with our own complicated life narratives and the long, multiple narratives of our cultural history. All of that is, at its heart, an *interpretive* process. In this chapter we sketch the bare outline of an anatomy of that process of interpretation, trying to learn as much as we can about its earliest stages.

Two Dialogues

Let us begin by looking at two very familiar dialogues in the Gospels. The first, from the Fourth Gospel, is not about Jesus directly but about John the Baptist.

> And this is the testimony of John, when the Judeans, priests and Levites, sent a delegation from Jerusalem to ask him, "Who are you?" And he confessed; he did not deny but confessed, "I am not the Anointed One." And they asked him, "What then? Are you Elijah?" And he said, "I'm not." "Are you the Prophet?" He answered, "No." Then they said to him, "Who are you?—that we can give an answer to the ones who sent us; what do you say about yourself?" He said, "I am a voice crying in the wilderness, 'Make straight the path of the Lord,' as Isaiah the prophet said." (John 1:19–23, my translation)

The questioners are frustrated by John's negative answers, and so perhaps are we, if we are fresh listeners to this rather strange tale. Neither they nor we find out who John is, and their further challenge, "Well, why are you baptizing then, if you are not the Anointed One nor Elijah nor the Prophet?" also receives no straightforward answer. "I am baptizing with water," he says. "In the midst of you stands one whom you do not know, the one who comes after me, the very thong of whose sandals I am not worthy to untie" (vv. 25–27). The next day John will name that unknown one, but still with cryptic words: "Behold the Lamb of God, who is taking away the sin of the world" (v. 29). And the day after that, John will point him out to two of his own disciples, who promptly transfer their allegiance to Jesus.

So the story of John's interrogation by Pharisees from Jerusalem is not about John after all; it is about Jesus. The evangelist labels it "John's testimony." The attentive reader learned already, in that prose note inserted into the wonderful poem that serves as the "Prologue in Heaven" to the Gospel, that John's whole existence was solely "in order to bear witness about the light." "He was not that light" (vv. 6–8). In the intricate literary tapestry which the anonymous singers, reciters, and writers of the Johannine community have produced, John's identity is a kind of negative space. The role of his character is like the function of negative space in a painting: to draw the eye of the viewer into the structure of the composition, setting off the limits, and ultimately leading us to participate in the active discovery of the mysterious, emerging whole of line, color, and shape. In the Fourth Gospel, John is there to make space for Jesus: "He must increase," he says, "I must diminish" (3:30).

But the Jesus to whom John yields space by his negations in this Gospel remains himself mysterious. "Among you stands one whom *you do not know*" (1:26). Notoriously, the characters who meet Jesus in the Johannine story are repeatedly flummoxed by his answers to their queries, baffled by the questions, Where does he come from? and Where is he going? and Who is he? Again and again, when he answers with a double entendre, they grab the wrong end of the stick and are left looking foolish. In part this is delightful for the reader. We learn enough on the first pages to feel a bit superior to these foolish interlocutors. And yet . . . are we really sure we get the point? The disciples themselves, surely our stand-ins in the narrative, do not fare much better than the outsiders and enemies, and people who want to believe are likely as not to be pushed into the darkness of incomprehension by some particularly sharp or absurd saying of Jesus.

What then are we to make of all those things John said he was not? Is Jesus everything John isn't—Anointed One, Prophet, Elijah? Further on, we shall come back to the question, where do all these characterizations come from? What meaning could it have had in first-century Roman Palestine to ask, "Are you the Prophet?" Who or what was "the Anointed One"? How could someone be Elijah, a prophet who disappeared from the scene nearly a millennium earlier? But first a note on the way these names, roles, or identities play out in the story of Jesus in John's Gospel. Of all of these possibilities of his role in the story, and several others besides, it has to be said, he is and he is not that. He is the Messiah, the anointed one, but this story defines who the Messiah is—not the other way around. Jesus does what Elijah does, but he is not Elijah come back from wherever the whirlwind took him (1 Kgs. 2:1–12).[1] Jesus is the final prophet, but no other prophet ever spoke like this (4:19, 44; 6:14–15; 7:40, 52; 9:17). He is the king of Israel, but he reigns not in war against the occupiers but in speaking the truth that the world cannot hear and therefore giving up his life for the dark world (John 18:33–38). This tension, between deep engagement with the symbols, personages, and stories of the traditions and Scriptures of Israel and the exuberant freedom to recast them all in the light of something radically new, is at the center of that *interpretive process* that we are trying to understand, the heart of the process by which Jesus' identity is discovered and invented by his early followers.

That same tension is apparent in a second passage, the famous story of the conversation between Jesus and his disciples as they walk toward Caesarea of Philip, often regarded as the very center of the plot of Mark's Gospel:

> And on the way [Jesus] asked his disciples, "Who do people say that I am?" They said, "John the Baptist, but others [say] Elijah, others, one of the prophets." Then he asked them, "And you—who do you say I am?" Peter up and said to him, "You are the Anointed one." But he warned them to tell no one about him.
>
> And he began to teach them that it is necessary for the Son of the Human to suffer many things, and to be rejected by the elders and the high priests and the scribes, and to be killed, and after three days to arise. He spoke this word to them with all candor. Then Peter grabbed him and began to rebuke him. But he turned and looked at the disciples and rebuked Peter. He said, "Get out of my way, you Satan. Your thinking is not God's, but all too human." (Mark 8:27–33, my translation)

In a way this little story is a positive countertype to the Fourth Gospel's story about John the Baptist. In contrast to the indirection of that episode, in which all John's negations pointed away from him and toward Jesus, this is directly about Jesus' identity, and Jesus himself asks the questions. Yet this story, too, has a largely negative and unfinished result. Like the interrogation of the Baptist, here too a variety of possible identities are being tried on for size, and none of them quite fits. We begin with outsiders' appraisals of Jesus, which the narrative implicitly rejects by Jesus' contrasting question to the disciples, "And you— who do you say I am?" Then the disciples are on the spot, and Peter, as so often, pipes up with what ought by the shape of the story to be the right answer. In Matthew's version of the same story, it quite clearly *is* the right answer, and earns Peter a special blessing (Matt. 16:16–19). But not according to Mark! Instead of being congratulated and renamed the Rock, Peter a minute later gets called Satan, the Opponent, the Tempter. Yet *Christos*, "Messiah," "the Anointed One" clearly *is* one of the names by which the community represented by this Gospel knows Jesus. Here again that interpretive tension surfaces, the tension that runs through the whole process by which Jesus gets named, and which these two Gospel writers have made central to their extraordinary narrative techniques.

Culturally Fashioned Roles

In every culture there are certain familiar roles played by characters in the standard life narratives of people in that culture: teacher, farmer, engineer, factory worker, builder, short-order cook, mother, husband, doctor, nurse. In the Gospel narratives we see Jesus in many of the roles that were typical of his time and place. Some of them are common throughout the Mediterranean world of antiquity; others are specific to Jewish culture. These roles reveal themselves not only in the things Jesus is called, but also in typical things he does. So he is a miracle worker, a healer; some would say, a magician. He is a sage who reveals his wisdom in pithy sayings, a prophet who speaks in a special genre of pithy saying in the name of God. People wonder if he is some figure of the past redivivus: Elijah come back from heaven or John the Baptizer risen from the dead. He is declared a king; his death looks like that of a martyr.

Where do such roles come from? Some spring from paradigmatic figures from a people's recited past: Socrates or Moses, Elijah or Diogenes or Jeremiah or Crates. For the Greeks Homer provides a catalogue of heroes and antiheroes that live on in popular rhetoric and biography. For the Jews, in a more intense and specific way, Torah and Prophets provide the grist for the mill of identity.

I have said that the whole interactive process by which Jesus becomes who he is for those who follow him is an interpretive process. The interpretation takes many forms, but one is absolutely central to the process: the interpretation of Jewish Scripture. The more we learn about the variety of ways in which different groups of Jews in the first century discovered meaning for their life in their world by artful interpretation of their Scriptures, the better we can understand how the identity of Jesus Christ was shaped in those early communities of his followers.

Clues from Qumran

Since the first Dead Sea Scrolls were discovered in 1947, we have known that these two-thousand-year-old manuscripts had the potential to transform the common understanding of both the Jewish forms of life in Roman Palestine and the emergence of the new sect that would come to be called "Christians." Some of the hypotheses about Christianity's relation to the group that used or produced the scrolls have been wildly fanciful, and almost everything about the scrolls remains controversial.[2] Nevertheless, there is a broad consensus, among those who know the manuscripts best, about their main features, and those features provide us with some informative parallels to the problem at hand.

The scrolls clear away one piece of misinformation that has distorted almost all modern attempts to explain the formation of Jesus' identity. Too often we have assumed that Judaism in the first century had, in effect, a standard set of dogmas about the Messiah or, more generally, a standard scenario about things that were to happen at the end of time. The problem of Jesus, then, boiled down to the question whether he actually did and said the things that the Messiah, or the Final Prophet, or the Son of Man (if there was such a figure), was supposed to do. This pattern of thinking is really only a thinly disguised version of a Christian apologetic strategy that goes back to the first century. Its first clear appearance is in the Gospel according to Luke and the Acts of the Apostles. In that two-volume work, the first sustained work of apologetic historiography by the early Christians, Jesus is proved to be the Messiah by a straightforward syllogism, repeated over and over: Scripture says that the Messiah must do x; Jesus did x; therefore Jesus is the Messiah.[3] There were a number of reasons for doubting the historical validity of this schema long before the discovery of the Dead Sea Scrolls, but that discovery very directly introduces us to a much more complicated picture. Those long-hidden manuscripts show us a group whose organization and ideology quite blithely cross the boundaries between kinds of Judaism that modern scholars have defined as antithetical: apocalyptic and halakhic, mystical and pragmatic, traditional and innovative, even perhaps Palestinian and Hellenistic. Instead of a fixed dogmatic system, we see a range of ways of imagining the hoped-for transformation from the present evil age to the age of righteousness, a changeable variety of leading characters in that final scenario, and evolving strategies for locating the community's own experiences within their imagined picture of the world. Perhaps most important, we see something of the internal process by which those scenarios were conceived and applied. There are three things we see happening in the scrolls that are parallel to tasks that the early Jesus movement had to accomplish. First, appropriate images had to be found to express the significance of charismatic figures. Second, certain "loaded" texts of Scripture, construed as prophecies, had to be explained and applied to the group's experience. Third, traumatic or scandalous events demanded explanation, by placing them within some convincing narrative of what God was doing in the world.[4]

The Teacher of Righteousness

Several of the texts from Qumran tell us about a person who was apparently the key organizer of the movement in its early years. For example, in the document known as the Damascus Covenant, first found in two incomplete medieval copies in the storeroom of a Cairo synagogue and then in fragments at Qumran, we read a tantalizingly brief account of the sect's beginnings:

> At the moment of wrath, three hundred and ninety years after having delivered them up into the hands of Nebuchadnezzar, king of Babylon, he [sc. God] visited them and caused to sprout from Israel and from Aaron a shoot of the planting, in order to possess his

land and to become fat with the good things of his soil. And they realised their sin and knew that they were guilty men, but they were like blind persons and like those who grope for the path over twenty years. And God appraised their deeds, because they sought him with a perfect heart, and raised up for them a Teacher of Righteousness, in order to direct them in the path of his heart. (CDC-A, 1.5–11)[5]

The scrolls in fact tell us very few details about this *moreh ha-ṣedeq*, "Teacher of Righteousness" or perhaps "Righteous Teacher" or "Legitimate Teacher." Despite his pivotal role in establishing the sect, he clearly did not occupy so unique or central a position in the movement's ideology as Jesus did for his followers. We have from Qumran no biographical accounts, no Gospels; we do not even know the name of the Teacher of Righteousness. Nevertheless, the salient features of the Qumran documents' spare descriptions of him do suggest some ways of thinking about the emergence of Jesus' Christian identity.

First, the designations of the Teacher of Righteousness are mostly functional. That is, it is his actual role within the community that he organized that suggests the epithets applied to him, rather than some preconceived ideology. On the other hand, his functions are so imagined and named that they bring to mind determinative episodes in the traditions and Scriptures of Israel. The renewal of the Sinai covenant is at the center of the sect's self-understanding, as we see most clearly in the ceremonies prescribed in the Rule of the Community. Not surprisingly, then, the Teacher of Righteousness bears many of the features of Moses; like Moses, he is for the community prophet, priest, and definitive interpreter of Torah.

Second, the role the Teacher has played in the community is described by allusions to Scripture and by direct exegesis of some texts. The interpretation of Scripture at Qumran is quite punctilious about selected details of the texts and yet at the same time quite free in lifting them out of both historical and literary contexts to apply to the group's own time and place.

Finally, the interpretation is eschatological in the sense that the very particular applications of biblical epithets, institutions, and prophecies to the sect and its own immediate historical context are authorized by the belief that they are living at "the end of days." The Rule of the Community, the Rule of the Damascus Covenant, and the various commentaries on particular scriptural books that are found among the scrolls all show us a sect that wants to re-create in its own life a repristinated biblical Israel. But their reading of the Bible that provides them the prescriptions for this form of Israel's life is itself refracted through the group's own special experience. For example, a famous passage in their commentary on the biblical prophet Habakkuk tells us that

> God told Habakkuk to write what was going to happen to the last generation, but he did not let him know the end of the age. And as for what he says, "So that the one who reads it may run," its interpretation concerns the Teacher of Righteousness, to whom God has disclosed all the mysteries of the words of his servants, the prophets. (1QpHab 7.1–4)[6]

Problematic Texts

A second generative factor we see in the Qumran sect's developing ideology is texts that seemed pregnant with meaning, yet whose plain sense was contradicted by the facts of history. For example, the words of the prophet Nathan, reported in 2 Samuel 7:11–14:

> The LORD declares to you that the LORD will make you a house. When your days are fulfilled and you lie down with your ancestors, I will raise up your off-spring [lit., "seed"] after you, who shall come forth from your body, and I will establish his kingdom. He shall build a house for my name, and I will establish the throne of his kingdom forever. I will be a father to him, and he shall be a son to me.

Presumably the prophecy was first taken to apply to Solomon, but Solomon's kingdom, far from lasting "forever," fell apart immediately on his death. For a nation that had suffered under the hegemony of the Seleucids and then the Romans, whose only kings in recent memory had been the Hasmonean priest-kings and the Roman puppet Herod, the unfulfilled prophecy could seem a cruel mockery. The solution, of course, was an eschatological fulfillment, as we hear in this fragmentary text from Qumran: "This (refers to the) 'branch of David,' who will arise with the Interpreter of the law who [will rise up] in Zi[on in] the last days, as it is written: 'I will raise up the hut of David which has fallen' . . ." (4QFlor1:10–12).[7]

Another text that was intriguing and problematical was Deuteronomy 18:15–18, where the promise is given that the Lord will raise up a prophet *like Moses*. Perhaps because the same book ends with the flat statement, "Never since has there arisen a prophet in Israel like Moses, whom the LORD knew face to face" (Deut. 34:10), this text, too, was ripe for eschatological interpretation. It became fundamental to the hopes of the Samaritan community, while to the Qumran sectaries it contributed the expectation of the coming, at the end of the present age, of "the prophet . . . and the Messiahs of Aaron and Israel" (1QS 9.11).[8] Both texts were important, too, to the early followers of Jesus.

Troublesome Events

A third factor that stimulated the Qumran group's interpretive activity was the brute challenge of startling or unpleasant events. For example, the clash between the official priesthood in Jerusalem and the sect, with their rival calendar, led to a confrontation on the day when the sect, but not the Temple, celebrated Yom Kippur. The group found that outrage cryptically predicted in the book of Habakkuk, in the words, "Woe to anyone making his companion drunk, spilling out his anger! He even makes him drunk to look at their festivals!" (Hab. 2:15). This, they said, "concerns the Wicked Priest who pursued the Teacher of Righteousness to consume him with the ferocity of his anger in the place of his exile, in festival time, during the rest of the day of Atonement" (1QpHab 11:2–7).[9] Similarly an inner schism, led by a rival to the Teacher of Righteousness, found its explanation in scriptural texts about the perversion of justice, while the alarming power of the rising Roman Empire was predicted in texts that originally spoke of Babylonia.[10]

Ritual, Poetry, and Midrash: The Christological Process

We are now ready to turn back to our main question: what was the process by which the emerging movement of Jesus' followers discovered an identity for him that turned themselves into "Christians" and him into the Christ, the

Son of God, the Lord, the eternal Word? This was, of course, a very complex and lengthy process, partly hidden from us by the scarcity of early sources; we can only consider a few illustrative examples.

The Crucified Messiah

If the Qumran group's interpretive strategies had to deal with events that challenged their belief in a God-ordered universe—opposition by the wicked priest, betrayal of the Teacher of Righteousness by some of his own followers, the unmerited success of the Roman forces—how much more the first followers of Jesus. The brute fact with which they had to cope was the public execution of their leader. The Roman prefect provided a sarcastic label for the crucified: "the king of the Jews." A warning: this was what happened to native insurrectionists who dared challenge Rome's hegemony. It was certainly what happened to all those royal and prophetic pretenders that Josephus catalogs for us.[11] The Jewish historian describes a long series of uprisings that challenged Roman occupation from the time the area was reorganized under the senatorial province Syria in 6 CE until the disastrous revolt of 66–73, in which Josephus himself was a participant. In each case the Roman prefect sends out troops to seize the ringleader, execute him conspicuously as an object lesson, and disperse the followers. In every case, destroying the leader was sufficient to send the followers scurrying into oblivion.[12] If some of the followers of Jesus chose rather to see Pilate's placard as unwittingly prophetic, if they formed the improbable conclusion that the crucified one was indeed the king of Israel, the truly anointed king of the end-time, then they faced a massive hermeneutical dilemma: interpret or despair.

The movement did not despair. For the earliest formative remnant of them the paradoxical notion that God's anointed vice regent was ignominiously killed became the generative center of their beliefs.[13] How was this interpretive tour de force possible?

The fundamental interpretive move was sublimely simple: God had overruled Pilate's action by raising the crucified messiah from the dead. Within a scarce twenty years of the event, the story was rehearsed in a lapidary formula of neatly balanced lines: "Christ died for our sins according to the scriptures and was buried; he was raised on the third day according to the scriptures and appeared." Then follows an extendible list of witnesses: "to Cephas, then to the Twelve, then he appeared to more than five hundred brothers at once, of whom most remain till the present, though some have died; then he appeared to James, then to all the apostles." And Paul, who is quoting the formula as a tradition he received and handed on to the Corinthian converts, adds "and last of all . . . he appeared to me" (1 Cor. 15:3–8, my translation).

Several things are evident from the formula. First, the identity of Jesus as God's anointed, as Messiah, is inextricably connected with his death. It is not that Jesus has fulfilled a role assigned by tradition to the Messiah and is therefore named such—as we see from Qumran, tradition did not even agree on a single Messiah. The futile scholarly searches for evidence in Jewish lore of a suffering Messiah are quite beside the point: it is because in Pilate's sarcasm and in the paradoxical belief of those first visionaries Jesus died as king of the Jews that he is named Messiah.[14] Therefore the notion of the Messiah itself is transformed.

Second, the process of assigning meaning to the scandalous event is a self-involving process. The formula states that Jesus "died for our sins." The absurdity of a crucified messiah becomes intelligible as a vicarious death for others. The community taking shape around this belief identifies its own fate with that death and that envisioned resurrection. Out of the dramatic ceremony of eschatological cleansing that John the Baptist had introduced, they create a ritual of initiation: they are baptized "into Christ." And they construe that transformation as dying and being buried with Christ so that they, too, may rise with Christ. The vicarious death is made ritually also an inclusive death.[15]

Third, meaning is inferred "according to the scriptures." The very earliest forms of the story of the crucifixion itself incorporate the language of Scripture. The graphic details that lend such verisimilitude to the passion narratives are drawn from the Psalms of Complaint: "Those who passed by wagged their heads at him," "they gave him vinegar to drink," "they divided his garments among them and for his clothing they cast lots," and even the "Last words" of Jesus according to Mark, "My God, My God, why have you forsaken me?"[16]

The Heavenly Human Figure

It was not the case that the early Christians simply took over texts of Scripture that were already taken to refer to the Messiah and applied them to Jesus. As we have seen, there was no standard ideology of messiahship. To be sure, the believers in Messiah Jesus made use of existing interpretive traditions of all kinds, when they were useful. For example, the prophecy that David's seed would be king forever and that he would be called God's son, which we found at Qumran to be forced into the future hope of an anointed king, was extremely convenient for

the early Christians.[17] Paul assumes the tradition in iden-
tifying Jesus with the seed of Abraham to whom the ultimate blessing of the Gentiles was promised, and the
author of Hebrews uses it to show the superiority of Jesus
even to angels.

The Scripture text that the New Testament writers
quote more often than any other is the first verse of Psalm
110 (LXX 109), which says in the Greek version, "The
Lord said to my lord, 'Sit at my right hand until I place
your enemies as a footstool beneath your feet'" (my translation). It sounded ready-made for the early interpreters
of the shameful crucifixion of Jesus. The defeat of the
Messiah is only a temporary illusion; in the reality knowable only to believers, God has exalted him to share God's
own rule in heaven until all his enemies are defeated.[18]

This text also illustrates another factor that we saw in
Qumran exegesis, and which often appears in other forms
of Jewish interpretation of Scripture: a text that has some
problematic or paradoxical feature tends to generate
interpretive ingenuity. Here the problem appears in the
Greek translation of the Psalm, in which (at least in some
versions) both *yahweh* and *'adōn* are translated by *kyrios*,
"lord." So how can there be two "lords" in heaven? The
hyperbole of the royal poet thus becomes a problem for
monotheistic theology and a wonderful opportunity for
the early Christians. This is only one of a variety of texts
that gave trouble to the rabbis and other Jewish interpreters who worried about the heretical notion that there
could be "two powers in heaven." Alan Segal has given us
a very nice account of some of the intricacies of the traditions and polemics that resulted.[19] A few of those texts
were particularly important to the Christians.

In a sense the classic case is in the first chapter of the
Bible. In the priestly story of creation, "God said, 'Let us

make a human being in our image and after our likeness'"
(Gen. 1:26, my translation). The "us" and "our" were
bothersome, but one could after all understand something
like a royal plural. Still, what was this human image that
belonged to Elohim and that was the archetype of humanity? The puzzle grows more complicated when the close
listener to the Bible's stories observes a certain contradic-
tion. On the one hand, we are told that "No human shall
see [God] and live" (Exod. 33:20, my translation). Yet earlier in the same book we hear that "Moses and Aaron,
Nadab, Abihu, and seventy of the elders of Israel went up,
and they saw the God of Israel," that they "ate and drank"
in God's presence, all apparently without harm (Exod.
24:9–11). And what was one to make of Isaiah's flat asser-
tion, "I saw YHWH" (Isa. 6:1)—and a similar report by
Micaiah (1 Kgs. 22:19), not to mention the elaborate
visions of Ezekiel (1; 10) and Daniel (7:9–14)?

Jewish exegetes found various solutions to the dilemma
of these texts. Those solutions are intriguing and often
delightful, but to pursue them in detail would take us away
from our immediate aim. Here the point is only the exu-
berance with which the early followers of Jesus made use
of them in their quest to understand just who he was and
who, if they were to believe in him, they were to be. When
Paul was converted to this sect of the crucified messiah,
the sect he had fiercely opposed, he was initiated by a ritual of baptism into Christ. Already, or at least by the time
he wrote to the Galatian converts a couple of decades
later, that ritual represented Christ as the very image of
God who had been the pattern of Adam's creation, and to
clothe oneself with Christ, as one rose from the burial-
waters of baptism, was to put on again that image, the garment of light that Adam and Eve had lost through their
disobedience, replacing that "garment of skin," the body

God had given to fallen humanity, the "old anthropos" that died with Christ in baptism. Jesus, the poetry said, was that heavenly anthropos, that second lord, that self-expression of the one God.[20]

The Continuing Interpretive Process

Here we have examined only a couple of samples of the multiple roles and images that became parts of the identity of Jesus among the adherents to his cult in the first century. We have focused not on the ingredients and antecedents of those roles and images, but on the process of identity formation. It was a ragged and sometimes self-contradictory process that does not lend itself to simple explanations. The interpretation of the Scriptures of Israel was central to the process, but it was also a process by which the followers of Jesus were trying to interpret their world, their experience, their own identity.

It is also a process that has no end as long as church and world continue. What counts as Scripture grows and changes and gets redefined and, eventually, is regularized into a canon that will include not only the Scriptures with which the first followers of Jesus began—those Scriptures which they shared with other Jews—but also some of the things they wrote, products themselves of that process of interpretation and reinterpretation. Struggling to find some order and some limits in the proliferation of inter-pretive possibilities—and of possible ways of living in the world whose history had a new pivotal chapter—leaders of the emerging churches tried to construct some guide-lines. The Rule of Faith and the Rule of Truth provided limits and rallying points, but also points of contention. Different ways of reading the Scriptures were identified: the literal reading stood over against the spiritual, and the spiritual could take several forms for several purposes. In the fifth century John Cassian delineated three of them as the tropological (or moral), the anagogical (which might have either a mystical or an eschatological drift), and the allegorical.[21] Many voices would contend in these developments, and every age produced new points of tension and new ways of rereading what previous interpreters had done. The discipline of philosophy with its changing fashions and the prudential dogmatics of mainstream church authorities would struggle with many forms of popular religion and faith, and always politics of both church and empire would throw its weight around. The struggle between clarity and confusion, between the necessity to make sense in a continually changing world and the passion to be faithful to foundations once laid, was and is unending.

In many ways those struggles can be glimpsed *in nuce* already in that master interpreter of the first generation, the apostle Paul. The next chapter examines the way in which Paul transformed the story of Jesus' death into the master metaphor for Christian life and thought, a story to think with.

Chapter Four

A Story to Think With
From Crucifixion to Metaphor

The previous chapter described one aspect of that complex interpretive process by which Jesus becomes who he is. It focused on some of the ways by which the early followers of Jesus found in their Scriptures images and patterns and stories with which they could make sense of Jesus. Most of those early interpreters are, for us, anonymous. But there is one whom we know rather well—though the more we know of him, the more puzzling he is—the apostle Paul.

One of the reasons Paul has been so puzzling is that we have tried so often to confine him in the straitjacket of the systematic theologian. Then we become upset about his apparent inconsistencies and self-contradictions. For the properly trained historical critic, Paul's use of Scripture is particularly appalling. He rips verses out of their contexts and insists that they mean something they could not possibly have meant to their original audiences. Where Scripture speaks clearly of the Torah, Paul announces with only a covert wink that it is really talking about Christ. Where the prophet speaks of an Israel that has temporarily become a nonpeople by its disobedience but by God's grace will again become God's people, Paul tells us he was really talking about the Gentiles to whom Paul has been preaching. There is no way Paul would ever pass a course in Old Testament Interpretation in one of our schools of theology.

Of course, we have also seen that leaders of the sect at Qumran were doing very similar things in interpreting Scripture. In different ways, many other groups of Jews also continued to develop free, ingenious, and varied procedures for finding in sacred texts guidance for the changing circumstances of their own lives. To a great extent, Paul was simply using the kinds of interpretive strategies typical of his time and place.[1] Recognizing that fact is a starting point for looking afresh at what he is doing, but only a starting point. We cannot interpret Scripture the way Paul did, but by seeing what he is doing in all its complexity, we do perhaps begin to suspect that there are other ways of thinking about Scripture and using it in the church than those that have dominated modern theology. (We return to these questions in the next chapter.)[2] However, there is another pole to the interpretive activity of Paul and other early Christians. While they were ingeniously using Scripture, as we saw in chapter 3, to interpret the death of Jesus and other things remembered about him, they were also using their Scripture-informed descriptions of Jesus to interpret their own experiences and the reality they encountered. In this chapter we focus on the latter kind of interpretation: the way Paul uses the story of Jesus' death and resurrection to interpret life and the world. We will see Paul not as a systematic theologian, but as a master of metaphor.

Trying to make Paul into a systematic theologian is a prime instance of that "Cartesian anxiety" that Ron Thiemann discerns behind much theology as well as much literary criticism today. Its hallmark is the assumption that a text must either be absolutely clear, with one univocal meaning, or it is absolutely indeterminate. The quest for the systematic single meaning represents one pole of that dilemma. The flip side is that "hermeneutical relativism" of the postmodern critic, which finds all narratives "unfollowable," as Frank Kermode puts it. Neither one is realistic, Thiemann insists, and neither one will work on Paul. The really interesting narratives are the ones that engage us to follow them into complexity and paradox. Tensions and contradictions are manifest in such a narrative because there are tensions and contradictions in this fallen world. The truth that such a narrative wants to tell us is not a single and uncomplicated doctrine, but a reality that always lies beyond our grasping.[3] That's the kind of narrative that Paul helped to construct. To do that, he became a master of metaphor.

In everyday speech, "metaphor" gets a bad rap. Speaking at a gathering of New Testament scholars a few years ago, I said that Paul's great contribution to emerging Christianity was to transform the cross of Jesus into a metaphor of almost unlimited extension. Immediately one of my colleagues objected: "The cross for Paul is not a mere metaphor! It is a literal fact!" The giveaway in his response, of course, was the word "mere." "*Mere* metaphor," as if metaphor were always *less* than a literal description. My answer was, "Without metaphor, the cross is just two timbers nailed together."

The *Logos* of the Cross

The word *logos* in the Greek of antiquity was one of those wonderful chameleons of words, whose semantic range is so rich in possibilities. In rhetoric as in philosophy, it was a word to conjure with. New Testament scholars and

86   *Christ Is the Question*

theologians have written thousands of pages about the meaning of that first line in the Fourth Gospel, "In the beginning was the *logos*." The word could refer to everything from a speech, to a volume of a multivolume work (like the Gospel of Luke, Acts 1:1), to the human capacity to reason, to that invisible, divine fluid that, for Stoics, was the rational structure of all reality. You can be sure that when Paul contrasts the *logos* of the cross with human wisdom, at the beginning of his first extant letter to the Corinthians, he does not mean just talking about the cross. To that young congregation, hungry for rhetoric and status, squabbling among themselves over whose apostle had more buzz and who among themselves had greater spiritual gifts, Paul says, "As for me, when I came to you, brothers and sisters, it wasn't with an effusion of rhetoric or of wisdom that I came declaring to you the mystery of God. For I had decided to know nothing among you except Jesus Christ—and him crucified" (1 Cor. 2:2–3, my translation).

There is another place in this letter where Paul reminds the new converts in Corinth of his first preaching to them, at the beginning of chapter 15. There he calls the message, as the earliest followers of Jesus habitually did, "the news," *to euangelion*, "the gospel," and he sums it up with a tight formula that he specifically identifies as a tradition he gave to them "among the first things":

> Christ died for our sins
>> according to the Scriptures
>> and he was buried
> and he was raised on the third day
>> according to the Scriptures
>> and he appeared to Cephas, then to the twelve . . .
>>>>> (15:3–5, my translation)

That's the story. Not very elaborate, when reduced to its bare essentials as in this formula, but the plot is direct, shocking, and powerful. Paul could cite a more developed version of it, in that chant we noted in chapter 2:

> [Hymn] the anointed Jesus,
> who had the very shape of God
> but did not count it windfall
> to be God's equal,
> but emptied himself,
> taking shape of slave:
> becoming of human likeness
> and found in human guise,
> he humbled himself—
> obedient to point of death:
> yes, of the cross's death.
>
> Therefore God has raised him high,
> conferred on him the name
> that's higher than every name,
> so at the name of Jesus
> every knee must bend:
> heavenly and earthly and infernal all,
> and every tongue must loudly own
> the Lord is Jesus Christ,
> to the glory of Father God.
> (Phil. 2:5–11, my translation)

How much of the narrative of the passion, as we know it from the later Gospels, did Paul know and how much of it did he recite to the congregations he founded? Certainly more than these summaries. In his reminder of the Last Supper, he mentions "the night when [Jesus] was betrayed" (1 Cor. 11:23), so the Christians in Corinth must have known a sequential narrative of some extent. Most often, however, a single phrase is enough in Paul's arguments to remind his audience of the "*logos* of the cross." To the Thessalonians, how "you turned from idols to serve the living God and to await God's son from heaven, whom he raised from the dead, Jesus who saves us from the wrath to come" (1 Thess. 1:9f.). Even briefer, "We believe that Jesus died and rose" (4:14). To the Galatians, how "before your eyes . . . Jesus Christ was publicly exhibited as crucified" (Gal. 3:1). What is significant is how pervasive these phrases are in all parts of Paul's writing, and how central they are to his vision of the form of life that the believers in Messiah Jesus ought to inhabit. A few examples illustrate the range of Paul's deployment of the motif.

Living Joyfully in a Nasty World

We begin with Paul's earliest letter that has come down to us—indeed the oldest Christian document of any kind that we can be sure of—the First Letter to the Thessalonians. Unlike most of the later letters, this one does not respond to a specific crisis. It is a letter of friendship. Like many letters to friends, it includes a note of consolation, a good bit of advice, some warnings, and a lot of reminders of things said and done between the friends when they were together. More than half of the letter recounts their first meeting, the things that have happened since, and Paul's own thoughts and feelings about them. Paul says that he has been worried about them since he left, wondering how their faith has stood up under the social tensions that inevitably follow from conversion to a cult. Eventually, when, as he says, "I couldn't stand it any longer," he has sent Timothy to check on them. In the let-

ter, when Paul recalls Timothy's return and his happy
report about the Thessalonians, he uses the verb that elsewhere we translate, "to preach the gospel"—*euange-
lizesthai*. "But now Timothy has just returned from his
visit to you, bringing good news of your faith and love. He
tells us that you always think kindly of us, and are as anx-
ious to see us as we are to see you. So amid all our diffi-
culties and hardships we are reassured, my friends, by the
news of your faith" (3:6–7, REB). It was "the good news,"
"our gospel" (*euangelion*) as Paul says earlier (1:5), that created this friendship. And the flourishing of this friendship
is good news, too. Paul uses the noun six times in this short
letter. And now he seems to be saying that this peculiar
friendship itself, with all its anxieties as well as its reliefs
and joys, is part of that good news, that gospel.

It has a shape to it, this gospel. There is a recurring
antinomy in Paul's account of his preaching it and their
receiving it and the life in fellowship that follows: "And
you became imitators both of us and of the Lord," says
Paul, "as you received the *logos* in much affliction, with joy
of the holy spirit" (1:6, my translation). *Thlipsis* and
chara—affliction and joy—these are the key words here.
Paul had sent Timothy to them, he says further on,
because he was concerned lest the affliction had been too
much for them. And Timothy was to remind them of what
Paul had told them from the beginning: "that we are destined to be afflicted" (3:3–4, my translation). For our purposes here, we need not debate just what kind of
"affliction" the Thessalonians had experienced. The
NRSV renders the word "persecution," but that is clearly
an overtranslation; there is nothing in the letter that
requires us to think of some kind of pogrom against the
Christian group in Thessalonica. What we do see, in 2:14,
is that they have suffered at the hands of their *symphyletai*,

their own kinsfolk or extended "tribe." And that is just what we would have expected. Whenever some members of a kinship group are converted to a foreign cult, typically their people become upset and may shun or attack them.[4]

Whatever the extent of the suffering, it is the model Paul gives to the converts for thinking about it that interests us. He defines their experience by setting it into a chain of imitation: in receiving the *logos* of the cross "with much affliction and with joy," they became imitators of Paul himself and of the Lord. Paul says a few words about his own afflictions: it was after having suffered and being assaulted in Philippi that he came to Thessalonica in the first place, but nevertheless by God he was given the bold speech that enabled him to speak to them "the gospel of God" (2:1–2). The subsequent stress they endured from their kinfolk also made the Thessalonian converts imitators of the congregations in Judaea (2:14). And in turn, they became a model, a *typos*, for "all the [new] believers in Macedonia and in Achaia" (1:7). Joy as a gift, in the midst of the suffering that inevitably comes to those who are enabled by faith to look directly into the face of the fallen world: that is the *logos* of the cross.

So is Paul's gospel after all just a variation on themes of sadomasochism? No. Neither Paul nor the converts in Thessalonica went looking for suffering; it happened because they exercised *parrhēsia*, boldness of speech in a world that resists truth in all its forms. Contrary to what seems the message in some modern films, the joy they were given by the Spirit had nothing to do with the pleasure, if that's what it is, of watching eyes gouged out and flesh flayed by whips. The *logos* of the cross is the rationality of the God who raised Jesus from the dead. It is the cross of the one who is *resurrected* that becomes the metaphor of life in the world.

The Old Is Dead; Freedom Lives

The language of imitation that Paul uses in 1 Thessalonians is dangerous. It tempts us to think that *we* do the imitating, that we can be like Jesus, and, if we are, God will take care of us and life will be just wonderful. It tempts us to think that the moral life can be summed up by such simple nostrums as, "What would Jesus do?" It tempts us to think that, if we take the pain, we'll get the gain. Paul, most emphatically, did not want to say that. The point he was making to the Thessalonians was that being like Jesus, being like Paul, being like the congregations in Judaea in discovering joy in the midst of stress was not an accomplishment—it was a gift.

Later, when Paul wrote to the congregations in Galatia, he faced a crisis in those churches, which revolved, as he saw it, precisely around the question, What must we do to be right with God? After Paul had left Galatia, some other apostles had come into those remote towns in Anatolia's central highlands to finish, as they said, the job he had started. All well and good, they said, that these Gentiles should now accept Jesus as Messiah, that, as a result of God's exceptional grace, these Gentiles should be incorporated into the people of God. They had taken the first step; God's spirit had manifested God's approval. Now they must complete their conversion: every male among them must be circumcised. It's the law. That's not our rule, it's God's rule. It's in the book.

Paul says, I know all about the book. I was a specialist. I know all about the law and the traditions and the rules and the righteous judgment against all those who don't keep them: I was a zealot (cf. Gal. 1:13–14). But something happened. Now "Neither circumcision nor a whole foreskin is anything: there is a new creation." Yes, a new creation, which Paul did not find or make, but which happened to him, because through Jesus Christ "the world has been crucified to me, and I to the world" (6:14–15). Extravagant language, but not careless. Paul is being quite deliberate, repeating here in his handwritten summary at the end of the letter a slightly different formulation that was a key to his argument earlier. There he had said: "For through the Law I died to the Law, that I might live to God. In Christ's crucifixion I was crucified. I live—but no longer *I*; rather Christ lives in me. The life I now live in flesh I live by the faith of God's son, who loved me and gave himself up for me" (2:19–20, my translation).

Paul, we would say, had a traumatic experience. Paul, we would say, was "born again." But it is not his experience that he is talking about. It is not his experience that the Thessalonian converts have imitated. After centuries of our modern subjectivism and individualism, immersed as we have been in sweet Pietism, heirs as we are to the Great Awakening and the tent meetings and the revival preachers and their commercial successors, the televangelists, it is hard for us to hear what Paul is saying. Of course he was changed. Of course his life turned 180 degrees. But those are merely symptoms of the real change: Paul's change is only a response to his discovery that the world has changed. There is a new creation, and that new creation was made by God through the dying and rising again of God's son, the Messiah. In that new creation, the rules God himself had given, the traditions for which Paul was zealous to the point of persecuting all who did not keep them, the very Book of God meant something quite new. The same Book of God that said, "Every male among you must be circumcised," also said, "A curse of God is everyone who is hanged on a tree" (Deut. 21:23, my trans.; cf. Gal. 3:13). The notion of a crucified Messiah was absurd.

The crucified was a curse, and either one must with all one's zeal try to stamp out that crazy idea, or one must acknowledge that God himself has rewritten the rules of his own Book. The absurd story of the crucified Messiah becomes for Paul the wedge by which the utterly New is driven into our world.

God's Foolishness in a Winner-Take-All World

In Corinth the converts to Paul's gospel had taken to the novelty that he preached with some enthusiasm. They were filled with the spirit. They prophesied. They received revelations. They worked miracles. They spoke in tongues. They sang new songs. Their weekly meetings were pretty noisy affairs, as Paul describes them (see 1 Cor. 14:26–40). Not everyone, of course, was pleased. The householders in whose homes these meetings were taking place, for example, may not have been completely happy when their slaves started declaring new revelations and even *women* had the audacity to prophesy (cf. 11:2–16). The normal hierarchy of the social order was being upset. At the meetings for the Lord's Supper, some of those normal distinctions of rank were reinforced by the hosts, and the resultant tensions were not pretty (11:17–34). The breakdown of family values threatened. Some were even saying that really spiritual people should live together without sex, while others said, "No, no, everything is allowed now—after all we're *spiritual* and sex only has to do with bodies: 'Food is meant for the stomach and the stomach for food, and God will destroy both'" (cf. 6:13). Some, the better off among them, kept up their social obligations by accepting invitations to dine in the temples of the numerous gods of Corinth; others were horrified: "That's idolatry!" they said. "Nonsense," said the temple-goers, "don't you *know* anything? Didn't you hear what Paul said? The news is, these gods aren't even real; we can do anything we want" (chaps. 8–10). To make matters worse, some people even objected to asking Paul's advice. They had met Apollos in the meantime, and he had charisma! What a speaker! What wisdom! They chose up sides: "I'm Apollos's man." "I'm Paul's." "Well, Cephas for me!" (chaps. 1–4). It was a mess.

In response, Paul wrote another letter to them. The first one, which had gone lost, was not very successful in straightening things out; they willfully misunderstood it and the divisions only got worse. So Paul wrote the long, carefully crafted letter we call 1 Corinthians. As Margaret Mitchell has shown, he adopts the tried and true rhetorical model of the speech for civic harmony. Harmony, *homonoia* was the central value of ancient Greek city life. Even today the main square in Athens is called "Homonoia Square" (compare Paris's *Place de la Concorde*). That is the word the ancient orators used for that proper order of things in the *polis*, when all the citizens and slaves knew where they belonged, all classes knew their place, those who naturally ruled and those who were naturally ruled. Like a body in which none of the organs was jealous of the others. Paul made his letter on that model; he even used some of the clichés, like that one about the body (chap. 12). But something was different, and what a difference.[5]

The motive that drove Greek and Roman society was *philotimia*, "ambition," literally "love of honor." It was a very stratified society, and honor went with status. Honor was public. Rich people gave money for public works, and in return they got big inscriptions on the buildings they paid for or the courtyards they paved and, sometimes, even a statue in a public place. They were elected to office, and they made more donations in return, and received more honor. Corinth was a little different from most of the older cities. It had been destroyed by the Romans in 146 BCE and lay desolate for a century before Julius Caesar refounded it as a Roman colony. We are told that many of the new colonists were freedmen—former slaves or children of slaves—and we can see in the surviving inscriptions how they rushed to assert themselves in this rare situation lacking the usual aristocracy above them. They made money and gave it away for big public buildings and placarded their names on them. One of them got promoted to one of the four highest offices of the colony, *aedile*. In return, he paved the plaza in front of the Theatre. His name was Erastos, and he was probably the same Erastos who, as treasurer of the city earlier, was one of the converts Paul was writing to.[6]

The point is, status was really important to the people who belonged to the little house churches of Jesus-followers in Corinth. And some of them, ordinary folks by the usual standards, had found in that new thing that Paul preached a new way of getting status—at least within the Jesus cult itself. They had the Spirit—and of course some had more Spirit than others. "My *charisma* is better than your charisma. *I* can speak in tongues!" "Your patron is Erastos? or Chloe? Well, mine is Paul." "But mine is Apollos." "*Mine* is *Jesus!*" No wonder Paul was exasperated; no wonder he resorted to sarcasm. "Look at your calling, brothers and sisters! Not many were wise according to flesh; not many big shots; not many of the aristocracy. But God chose the foolish things of the world to shame the wise, the weak things of the world God chose, to shame the powerful. God chose the vulgar things of the world and those despised, the nothings, in order to take down the somethings" (1 Cor. 1:26–28, my trans.).

The Corinthian Christians had understood that the gospel was about something new. They understood that

that newness affected the very way they lived their lives, that it mattered in the houses and workshops, the streets and temples and the *agora* of Corinth. It mattered in relationships; it mattered in status; it mattered in the longing for honor. Paul doesn't want to take any of that newness away from them. But their vision of the new is not yet new enough. They are taking the glory of the gospel as a way to get ahead in the old, winner-take-all world. What Paul wants them to see is that there is another world, a new creation. In that new world, the winner is the one who was crucified, who is glorious in his humility, who triumphs only in order to hand his kingdom finally over to God.

Not only do they have things to learn—especially those among them who are so proud of their spirit-given *gnōsis*, their "knowledge" and their "wisdom"—Paul is learning things, too, as he wrestles with their misunderstandings. He, too, is still living in the old world, as every one of us must do. He is using all the tools he knows of Greek language and rhetoric and philosophy to put into words that new thing that has happened in this old world.

We see a sign of Paul's own struggle in that exasperated topic sentence with which he introduces the theme of the letter: "I appeal to you, brothers and sisters, by the name of our Lord Jesus Christ, that you all say the same thing and that there not be schisms among you, that you be established in the same thought and the same opinion!" (1:10, my trans.). Now wouldn't that be wonderful! Everyone saying the same thing and everybody having the same opinion! Harmony indeed. I can imagine pastors silently wishing such a thing for their congregations: everyone in agreement, no conflicts, no arguments. But if they think for a minute, they know that they would not really wish that, and neither did Paul! Take, for example, the matter of the meat sacrificed to idols, which occupies chapters

8–10 of the letter. Everyone who reads this part of the letter honestly is likely to conclude that Paul couldn't make up his own mind. First he agrees with the Knowing Ones, that, of course, none of those images in the temples are real gods (8:4–6), but he reminds them that they are also responsible for those "weak" ones who do not share their knowledge (8:7–13). Yes, their knowledge gives them authority, but how does that authority affect other members of the community? Talk about authority, says Paul, look at the authority I have as an apostle to collect a salary and travel expenses—I'd rather die than *use* that authority, because it is in *giving up* that authority, slaving away with my hands, that I show my freedom. Yes, free from everyone, I became everybody's slave (as the ancients said of the demagogue!) in order to win over multitudes (chap. 9). Then he turns again and backs up the "weak" Christians' attack on idolatry by quoting the key passage on idolatry from the Torah and giving them a little midrash on it (10:1–13). Idols may not be real, but demons are, replies Paul, and you can't eat at both God's table and the table of demons (10:19–21). Then to the smart folks, Yes, everything is now allowed. You have authority to eat or not to eat. But not everything builds up the community (10:23). Only at the end to agree with the Knowing Ones that you can eat anything that's sold in the meat market, and backing that with a prooftext as well (10:24–30).

What is going on? Far from making everyone say the same thing, Paul has helped both sides speak up more clearly—especially those "weak" who, we may guess, were a lot less articulate than those who prided themselves on wisdom and knowledge. And he adds to the conversation a number of other voices as well: the voice of Scripture, the voice of tradition, the voice of convention, the voice of the community's own experience. But most of all, the strong voice of that central narrative that he called the good news, the *logos* of the cross. So we are not surprised that, at the end of his complex but masterful orchestrating of their many-voiced argument, he comes back to the motif that was so prominent in 1 Thessalonians: "Be imitators of me, as I am of Christ" (11:1).

Conclusion

The *logos* of the cross, for Paul, means more than just talking about Jesus' crucifixion. It means that, for those who have been seized by "the faith of Jesus Christ," the very logic of reality has changed. It is a new creation. That change can be expressed only by indirection, by metaphor.

The pivotal story for Paul was simple and astounding: God's son and anointed one was the very Jesus who was most shamefully crucified, dead, and buried, but whom God then raised from the dead, exalted to share his own throne and very name in heaven, to sit at God's right hand as Lord until all things would be subjected to him and God alone would reign in righteousness over all his people and creation. The drama of Paul's career turns on his recognition that that story shattered and re-created his own conception of a life lived in obedience of God's will. For him it equally shattered and re-created—but preserved!—Israel's fundamental reason for existing in the world as God's people. When Paul writes to the various communities that he founded, it is invariably to suggest, cajole, argue, threaten, shame, and encourage those communities into behaving, in their very specific situations, in ways somehow homologous to that fundamental story. In the process, Paul uses older stories and older rules, maxims, customs, and moral commonplaces to interpret the Christ-story—but simultaneously uses the Christ-story to transform those older stories, rules, maxims, customs, and commonplaces. That led to a certain polyphony in Paul's discourse: he lets many voices speak, and through that "dialogic imagination," to use Bakhtin's phrase, brings the master metaphor to bear on life.[7]

Paul's most profound bequest to subsequent Christian discourse was his transformation of that reported event into a multipurpose metaphor with vast generative and transformative power. Above all he saw revolutionary import for the relationships of power that, in every society, control human relationships. He works out this import not in a social theory but in his response to specific crises of leadership and dangers of schism within the Christian house-communities, especially at Corinth. If God's power is manifested in the weakness of the Cross, and God's wisdom in the foolish claim that the crucified was the Messiah, then it is no longer obvious that the high-born, wealthy, well-educated, rhetorically sophisticated should always have their way, while those who are socially "nothing," those who are "weak," the women, the slaves, the poor, the uneducated are simply to obey. To underscore the point, Paul hints at the story of his own life since his conversion, which God has made to conform to the story of the cross, forcing him to live by hope of the resurrection. "For I think," he says, "God has publicly displayed us apostles as the last, as people under death sentences, as a theatrical spectacle to the world of both angels and humans. We are fools for Christ's sake; you are clever in Christ. We are weak; you are strong. You are glorious; we are dishonored" (1 Cor. 4:9–10, my trans.). Yet he makes it plain that he is not talking about a simple inversion of values. Those who have no status or prestige in the households and assemblies of Corinth but only the ecstatic power given by the spirit of God may nevertheless also be guilty of being "inflated" by their own pseudo-knowledge and windy, tongue-speaking power. Thus Paul's use of the metaphor of the cross resists its translation into simple slogans. Instead he introduces into the moral language of the new movement a way of seeking after resonances in the basic story for all kinds of relationships of disciples with the world and with one another, so that the event-become-metaphor could become the generative center of almost endless new narratives, yet remain a check and control over those narratives.

If Paul is right, then the task of Christians to figure out what it is that God is calling us to do at a particular time and in a particular situation is not a simple one. Our next chapter confronts the claim that all the answers are in the Book, that "the Bible clearly teaches" all the things we need to know.

Chapter Five

The Bible Teaches . . . through a Glass Darkly

W henever I hear someone say, "The Bible clearly teaches. . . ," I am reminded of an experience I had very early in my days as a candidate for the ministry of the Presbyterian Church. I was only a junior in the University of Alabama, and I should never have been turned loose on an unsuspecting congregation, but a combination of the Presbytery's shortage of ordained pastors with the mutual economic convenience of the congregation and myself— they were too poor to pay a real minister and I so broke I took anything I could get—brought me together with a tiny, rural congregation near Northport, Alabama: the Bethel Presbyterian Church. They eventually fired me, in defiance or ignorance of all Presbyterian order, but rather later than I had expected, given our clash of expectations. By that time I had come to love them, and a few of them even came to love me. It was a learning experience for both sides. I'm not sure what they learned, but one of the things I learned was the astonishing array of ways the Bible holds authority among ordinary believers.

One Sunday, as early-comers chattered away before the

service began, one of our pillars declared that his favorite coon dog had just had puppies. Somebody asked him how much he was going to sell them for. "Oh," said he, "I can't do that. It says in the Bible, 'Thou shalt not take the price of a dog.'" There was silence, as all eyes turned to me, the student, the expert from the university, the preacher. And yet again, I failed them utterly. I said I didn't know that verse, and I'd have to look it up.

I did look it up. It really is there. In the King James Version of Deuteronomy 23:18, the Bible says, "Thou shalt not bring the hire of a whore, or the price of a dog, into the house of the LORD thy God for any vow: for even both these are abomination unto the LORD thy God." If I had been better of memory or quicker of wit, I could have set the puppy owner's mind at ease. As far as I know, he had not made any vow requiring to be paid in church, and in any case, if he did sell his puppies, as long as he kept the money out of the collection plate, it would seem the LORD God would not mind. Or I could have seized this as an educational opportunity, to preach about texts in their context. What was the "hire of a whore" doing in the same sentence with "the price of a dog"? Newer translations, of course, make things a little clearer. The Revised English Bible, for example, translates or rather paraphrases, "You must not allow a common prostitute's fee, or the pay of a male prostitute, to be brought into the house of the LORD your God in fulfilment of any vow." The new *Jewish Study Bible* keeps to a literal translation but adds a footnote to the same effect. In the event, however, I failed my little congregation at Bethel Presbyterian, and for all I know, they may still have trouble buying and selling coon dogs in that place—although, knowing their ingenuity in things of this world, I bet they worked out a barter arrangement pretty quickly.

The Trouble with the Literal

I admit the example is a little silly, but it really did happen, and it illustrates some of the problems hidden behind our debates over the "meaning" of Scripture. The issue may seem trivial, but the structure of the argument that was implied by my dog owner's scruples is not different from that mounted by many of those spokespersons who are so stridently and confidently proclaiming God's easy answer to the complicated problems we are facing in our national life today. "The Bible clearly teaches . . ."—you fill in the blank. And such arguments are taken seriously—sometimes with deadly seriousness—by many people.

Several tangled issues are present here, and our first step must be just to try to sort them out. To begin with, there is the problem of what is "literal." Accusing my dog owner of being too literal in his reading of Scripture is very easy. At one level that is surely true. "Literal" meaning at this level refers to something like the meaning you would arrive at if you had to look up every word in the dictionary and accepted the first definition provided. If you have tried to read the user's guide for a new electronic device produced in, say, Japan or South Korea, you know what that kind of translation looks like. The native speaker does not use language that way. Ordinary language careens happily between ostensive meanings and tropes of all kinds without any loss of the power to communicate. If I had said to my worried dog owner, "It's raining cats and dogs," I don't imagine for a minute that he would have rushed to the window to see if Persians, Maine Coons, Pekingese, and poodles were descending from the heavens. Within the community of competent speakers of a particular language, we understand that kind of code-shifting without thinking about it. Our everyday speech is crammed with metaphors, and a little common sense helps. It is to common sense that St. Paul implicitly appeals, as he cheerfully abandons the literal meaning of a text he is quoting from that same book of Deuteronomy, in order to make it say something altogether different: "Is it oxen that God cares about?" (1 Cor. 9:9, my trans.). Equally we might ask, commonsensically, "Is it the price of dogs that God cares about?" But wait a minute. I think the historical critic will likely say, "But in fact the compiler of the laws of Deuteronomy really did think God cared about oxen and their welfare." And perhaps she will go on to say, "And so ought we to care about the welfare of all living creatures, including not only oxen but also whales and, for that matter, dogs." Perhaps there are times when we ought to read "literally" and times when it is deeply misleading to do so. There are at least two problems, then, right here at the beginning: (1) "When is the literal really literal?" and (2) "How do we move from whatever the literal meaning is (or was) to that 'And so ought we'?"

From "Literal" to "Historical"

Let's go back to the "literal" meaning of Deuteronomy 23:18. How do we know that "dog" here does not mean a quadruped with a wagging tail, but instead is a slang term for a male prostitute such as were active in Canaanite fertility cults? We know that because of historical research into language usage. And that knowledge amounts to our persuasion, or rather the persuasion of the linguistic experts whose opinion we trust, that a native speaker of Hebrew in ancient Israel, hearing the phrase *mechîr kelev*, "price of a dog," side by side with the phrase *etnan zonah*, "fee of a prostitute," would immediately have understood that "dog," too, meant a kind of prostitute—in just the same way in which we know that "raining cats and dogs" means a very heavy rain, not that tabbies and beagles are falling from the sky. Making that kind of judgment is what modern biblical scholarship does. On the whole it does it very well. Mind you, the process can be very complicated, as all students of ancient Near Eastern languages or of Hellenistic Greek can attest, but the central idea is fairly simple: the plain or literal meaning of a text is what it would have meant in its historical setting to a competent native speaker of its original language. We shall come back to that notion, which is an important one. But first, let us notice how very modern it is.

For most of Christian history, about eighteen centuries in fact, the "literal sense" meant something quite different. The literal sense of a text was its face value to a reader or hearer who was formed by the Christian experience and the Christian story, by the church's liturgy, its creeds, its catechism, its hymns, its ethos. It was the plain meaning. A text might have other meanings as well, and for theologians and preachers these "spiritual" meanings might be even more important—the allegorical meaning, the moral, and the anagogical. But the plain meaning was there for all—all, that is, who had been socialized properly into the Christian community and its traditions. The literal meaning was an insider's meaning, but for the insider it seemed to reside in the text itself. From our point of view, that seems a benign sleight of hand, for in today's understanding of semantics the meaning, like all meaning, really lived in the field between the text and the community that used it, between text and audience. Meaning was transactional, but not consciously so. And it worked as the literal meaning precisely because the transactions were unconscious. The text meant what the text said.

Beginning early in the eighteenth century, as Hans Frei has pointed out, a change took place in the way texts, and all language, were understood to signify. This change follows the exaltation of the powers of reason by the Enlightenment and the glorification of objective observation by the new empirical sciences. The result, says Frei, is a radical simplification of meaning. "Concepts like 'fact,' 'probability,' and 'verification,'" he says, "turned all language into a mirror of reality or a perceptual report of our knowledge of what is extramental."[1] Real meaning becomes *ostensive* meaning, that is, a text means by *referring* to something outside itself: something in the "real" world, a thing, a fact, an event. Frei, of course, particularly laments the effect that this narrowing of meaning had upon the way in which we read narrative; indeed he speaks of the "Eclipse of Biblical Narrative."[2] Now the question whether a story is "true" or not turns into the question of whether the events the story narrates really happened that way. If we cannot believe that a great fish really swallowed Jonah and spit him out again unharmed, then there is no truth in the story. And whether we can believe the fish part of the story is a question to be settled by reason and by observation. Has anyone ever in fact seen a fish that could swallow a man whole? Is it rational to suppose that, if such a fish existed and if such a man were swallowed, said man would survive three days and three nights of confinement in the fish's stomach? In a rational universe, is it moral to suppose that the Creator would suspend all normal laws of biology and physics just to teach Jonah and the Ninevites a lesson? The change of focus affects equally the modernists and their opponents. The modernist looks at many things in the Bible and announces, with Sporting Life of *Porgy and Bess*, "It ain't necessarily so." And the fundamentalist responds, "Oh, yes it is!" This new episte-

mology creates a new kind of literalism, and you are either
for it or against it, but both sides are playing more or less
the same language game.

The way in which the new temper of the Enlightenment most directly affected biblical interpretation was
through the rise of modern historiography. The ideals of
rationality, universality, neutrality of perspective, and
objective verification—ideals that reigned in the new
physical sciences—naturally became the goals of scientific
history as well. Because so much of the Bible contains
accounts of things that are said to have happened in the
past, biblical scholars had to become historians. The most
fundamental of exegetical sciences, the study of language,
becomes a historical discipline, for language changes over
time, and what a word meant in Plato's time is not necessarily the same as what it meant in the common language
of Rome's eastern provinces four or five centuries later.
The literal sense of the text becomes the historical sense.
When the literal sense has become the historical sense, literalism has become fundamentalism, the only alternative
seems to be a knowing skepticism, and in the process what
had been the plain sense of the text has often been lost
from view.

The Triumph of the Expert and the Self-Defeat of Scripture's Clarity

The triumph of modern historicism is at the same time the
triumph of the expert. When the plain sense of the text
becomes the historical meaning, then two degrees of separation impose themselves between people like my naive
dog owner at Bethel Presbyterian and the text by which
they are trying to live. First, they have to live in a *now*
which is separated by a far greater distance than they

imagine from *then*. What the text *meant* is not necessarily, and indeed very often not, what it *means*. Second, because the ordinary readers lack the skills of the historical philologian and the historian of ancient society, they are separated from that expertise which has now become necessary to know the historical meaning of the text.

There is a very sad irony in this double separation. My dog owner had undoubtedly been taught, since he was a good Presbyterian, that every person ought to read the Bible for himself or herself and to try to live by its plain meaning. The conviction that Scripture is clear in itself has played a fundamental role in the development of those traditions that are rooted in the Protestant Reformation. The doctrine of the *claritas scripturae* was one of Luther's strongest weapons against the papacy and the whole hierarchy of the church arrayed against him. For if Scripture seemed obscure in itself—and many an innocent reader has thought it did—then it must be kept out of the hands of the naive reader. For that reader, the truths of Scripture must be distilled and filtered by those who were anchored in the safe tradition of the church's interpretation and who were authorized and legitimated by the church to teach that filtered truth. But if the essential truths of Scripture were clear in themselves, then any reader might say with Luther, "I do not accept the authority of popes and councils, for they have contradicted each other—my conscience is captive to the Word of God."[3] Insistence on *sola scriptura* as the rule for faith and life required, then, that one also embrace the doctrine of Scripture's clarity. So when Erasmus pointed out that there were rather a lot of things in Scripture that were less than transparent, Luther denounced him vehemently not only for his sophistic skepticism but for a position that supported the papacy. If there were things hard to understand in Scripture (as

Luther surely knew there were), then the fault did not lie in Scripture. It lay rather in the devil's wiles and our own sin.[4] Calvin, of course, agreed. All our powers of knowing have been corrupted by sin, so that we cannot know aright without the spirit's help.

The doctrine had its dangers, however, as the Reformers quickly saw. Both Luther and Calvin were quite impatient with those unruly prophets who sprang up around them, claiming to find by the spirit all kinds of novelties in Scripture and producing all kinds of disorder by their preaching. Evidently the clarity of Scripture was a bit tricky and depended a lot on who was doing the looking. As recent scholarly investigations of the doctrine of *claritas* have pointed out, it was a polemical doctrine from the outset, and the context determined its application.[5]

This tension between the plain sense of Scripture as defined by the common sense of the tradition, on the one hand, and, on the other, the untrammeled freedom of the individual interpreter, guided only by what the Spirit seemed to be saying in his or her heart, determined the future of interpretation down to our own day. This tension was magnified and altered by developments in the academy, on one side, and in popular culture, on the other.

The academic side of the story is one of the steady professionalization of biblical interpretation. On the face of it, there is nothing wrong with that. The Reformers were scholars, and indeed it can be argued that the scholarship of Renaissance humanism made the Reformation possible.[6] The mainstream heirs of the Reformation have always encouraged scholarship, and they were instrumental in the founding of many of the great universities and colleges in this country. From the doctrines of *sola scriptura* and *claritas scripturae* follow directly the immense and successful labors at translation of the Bible into ordinary languages that have gone on for five centuries. The Reformers thought the main cause of the Bible's obscurity was sin, but they also knew that even the purest saint could not understand what *mᵉchîr kelev* meant if she did not know Hebrew.

However, as we have seen in chapter 1, the peculiar form of academic professionalism that we know today drew deeply upon the emerging ideals of the Enlightenment and of modern science. For biblical scholarship, that meant, as we have seen, the redefinition of the enterprise as a division of scientific history-writing, and there followed the necessary methodological skepticism without which no historian can do her job effectively. The hermeneutics of suspicion is the air we breathe. There also followed a passionate devotion to the past as past, the determination to let the past speak for itself, be it ever so different from what we think it ought to have been or done or said. Now when that happens, when history is devoted to learning "how it really was," to the extent that this is possible, the historian will almost inevitably be at odds with any ongoing practice of using the story of the past for present goods. The more we succeed as historians, the more aware we are of the differences between past and present, and that abyss between then and now yawns before every would-be believer.

Moreover, professionalization, in the university as in our society in general, has meant specialization. When the University of Berlin was organized in 1810, it was intended to become a model of efficient application of Enlightenment principles in the modern world. And so it was. It was also a model of the best of Prussian bureaucracy.[7] The organization of learning into distinct faculties or disciplines has become the standard by which those of us all live who teach and learn in modern universities and colleges. "Divide and conquer" worked well for Caesar, and it works well for some kinds of learning. It also works well for the establishment of bureaucratic fiefdoms, as we all know very well indeed. Specialization enhances concentration and control. It makes possible sustained, intense effort on closely defined tasks, but it often separates us from just those people to whom we ought to be listening, and who might need to listen to us.

On the other side of the great divide, in popular culture, we have seen developments that also inhibit the free interchange between professional scholarship and lives of Christian laypeople. First, the radical individualism and subjectivism that have been characteristic of the modern Western world, whose influence on the academic ways of knowing we have already talked about, have also been deeply embedded in the popular ethos—perhaps more in North America than anywhere else on earth. So, as the evangelical scholar James Callahan has pointed out, "In nineteenth-century America perspicuity became a democratized affirmation of religious equality."[8] The Bible became the people's book, and with that came a suspicion of the expert which might have been a healthy antidote to that professionalization and compartmentalization mentioned above, but in practice leads to something close to anarchy in popular interpretation.

The tendency toward anarchy was intensified by two further characteristics of American religion that emerged strongly in the age of the Western frontier: pietism and anti-intellectualism. For the Pietist, the cure for Scripture's apparent obscurity lay in one's heart, not in one's brain. Ardor, not learning, passion, not thinking would make everything plain.

The religion of the heart need not be opposed to religion of the mind, but in our national experience it has lent itself readily to an alliance with anti-intellectualism. In the nineteenth century, as the frontier rolled westward, Presbyterians, for example, experienced that alliance acutely in the debates over the need for an educated clergy.[9] From the pragmatic concern that the settlers in the new territories would be left without any spiritual guidance if they had to wait for enough candidates to make it through seminary, there rather soon developed a persuasion in many quarters that preachers with advanced degrees were not just an expensive luxury but likely to be out of touch with the real lives of people. What could they know about the Bible if they didn't know about life? What was needed was not preachers with book-learning, but preachers who were born again, with the fire of the Spirit in their bellies. Thus the same Protestant tradition that gave to this country much of its zeal for education and many of its pioneering educational institutions also contributed to that pervasive anti-intellectualism that infects every part of our national life.

Meanwhile, the universities and other educational institutions began to discover a powerful tension between their Protestant roots and their roots in the Enlightenment. That earlier struggle for liberation of the soul of the believer from the Roman hierarchy now had its counterpart in the struggle for liberation of the mind of the scholar from the institutions of Protestant scholasticism. So if in many of the churches there persists a pervasive anti-intellectualism, in the universities there grows up a pervasive intellectual antireligionism.

The biblical scholar is caught in between. To the religious person outside the university, the biblical scholar's professionalization looks more and more like secularization. The success of historical research, which was supposed to make everything clear, instead serves only to make the Bible more and more obscure. The past recedes from our world. We learn how very different the ancient Israelites and the early Christians were from anything we experience. The biblical scholar's methodological skepticism is hard to distinguish from unbelief, and of course it may lead to the latter. Yet within the university, the biblical scholar remains in most cases completely isolated from colleagues in other departments, who are likely to regard his whole field of study as a relic from the Age of Superstition.

And so we get that peculiar schizophrenia that makes popular discourse about religion so bizarre in the present-day mass media. At one end of the spectrum are many self-styled evangelicals who make the "Left Behind" novels the best-selling books in the world. These Bible believers are embracing a peculiar kind of premillennialist narcissism, the roots of which lie in a heresy that was introduced in the early nineteenth century, the Dispensationalism of John Nelson Darby and his American followers.[10] For these believers, most of whom are deeply distrustful of professional biblical scholarship, this strange and complex fantasy story is the literal sense of the Bible. More bizarre, but fully understandable in today's political climate, is the cynical exploitation of this set of beliefs by neoconservative strategists, who see in the rather weird role played by a restored state of Israel in Dispensationalism's projection of the latter days a means to gain religious support for their imperial and thoroughly secular plans for the Middle East.

At the other end of the spectrum, we find the democratization of nineteenth-century modernist historical criticism. Thus every new archaeological or manuscript discovery is promoted in the mass media as finally offering us the key to understanding who Jesus really was and what really happened in early Christianity. If there is a hint of the sensational in the discovery, and if there can be added the possibility that the truth has been kept from us by a dark conspiracy of the institutional church, then the results are made for television or for the blockbuster best seller. Among the best known of these efforts to exploit the innocence of the mythical "intelligent layman" is the Jesus Seminar.[11] It turns out, of course, that the Jesus Seminar is perhaps the least irresponsible of such attempts to bring modern historicism to the masses. At least its publicists were genuinely trying to revive the mission of late-nineteenth-century historical criticism: to liberate the individual reader from the oppressive dogmas of institutional religion. That is, their aim is to restore the literal sense as the historical sense. In too many instances, as we saw in chapter 2, that has meant the history as reconstructed with some new piece of evidence or some particular hypothesis as the universal key. Many have followed in their train. By the time we come to Dan Brown's delightful fantasy, constructed with the novelist's delicious freedom to make up facts out of thin air, we are not surprised to find millions of readers prepared to believe that *The Da Vinci Code* actually reveals real secrets.

The history of the doctrine of the clarity of Scripture, the belief that the meaning of Scripture is transparent to the innocent reader, or the skillful reader, or the pious reader, thus seems to be the history of a self-consuming idea. The plain sense as it once existed, the common sense found in the text by the authoritative tradition, has vanished, and in its place is a chaotic puzzle to be decoded at the whim of whatever interpreter you may trust. The net result is that the situation warned against in the Letter to Ephesians rules popular religion in America: we are like "children, tossed to and fro and blown about by every wind of doctrine, by people's trickery, by their craftiness in deceitful scheming" (Eph. 4:14). The solution, Paul's disciple wrote, was to grow up. It is time to recognize that the doctrine of Scripture's transparency, which has served various polemical purposes in the history of doctrine, is not for grown-ups. The conceit that "the Bible clearly teaches" this, that, and the other thing is one of those childish things we ought to put away.

Trying to Rescue the Plain Sense

There have been a number of attempts in recent years to rescue the doctrine of Scripture's clarity, and with it the notion of the plain or literal sense of the text. For example, James Callahan, the evangelical scholar quoted above, is at pains to show that the doctrine has meaning only contextually. Its context is specifically the tradition of Protestant hermeneutics, and its function is to describe how the text works within the Protestant community. What is clear in Scripture is not any and every fact, viewpoint, or doctrine, but precisely that one central story that is essential for human salvation.[12]

That certainly moves in the right direction. Here Callahan is adopting much of the program that Hans Frei and several of his students, none of whom would call themselves evangelicals in Callahan's sense, have been working out. It was Frei who first suggested, as Kathryn Tanner puts it, that the *sensus literalis* of Scripture is a quasi-sociological category, "part of the self-description of the Christian community." Clarity is not a property of the text itself, but "a product of an interpretive tradition." Tanner goes on to suggest that, while such a way of thinking about interpretation looks very conservative on its face, it has in fact a built-in requirement for continual self-criticism. Her language is a little complicated, but I think it is worth quoting at length: "A tradition self-critical of its own specifications of the plain sense will arise . . . when the network of conventions that the plain sense helps to constitute turns back on that notion and complicates its function." Two factors are important: the practice of the canon, which, by limiting the Scriptures that are authoritative, implies that they have to be continually reinterpreted, and "the practice of classifying the plain sense of these texts under the rubric 'narrative.'" Classifying the plain sense as narrative is, of course, Hans Frei's distinctive turn—though he would have said he learned it from Karl Barth, who (David Kelsey once remarked) regarded the whole Bible as the first nonfiction novel. Tanner thinks that move saves the Bible from those ways of construing it that get people into the kind of dilemmas represented by my dog owner at Bethel. So long as the nature of the plain sense is defined as, say, teaching cultic acts or forms of behavior, as rules or regulations or theological concepts, then it tends to be construed as something timeless and unchanging. But narrative is by its nature at one step removed from the act of "applying" it to the situation of the community. "The formation of a Christian character is always set as a task, in other words, by such a structural indeterminacy in Christian conventions of appealing to texts."[13]

This perspective should be set alongside the crucial point made many years ago by David Kelsey, that the way the Bible is used in theology depends on the way the reader construes the Bible—that is, what one takes the Bible essentially to be.[14] My dog owner implicitly construed it as a giant and complex rule book. If it said you don't take the price of a dog into the House of the LORD, then you don't take the price of a dog into the House of the LORD—period. To be sure, even he could not be quite literal about it. Since the whole business about vows was incomprehensible, better forget that altogether and just avoid selling dogs. Never mind the selectivity into which every reader of the Bible as rule book inevitably falls. For example, it would never have occurred to my dog owner, or anybody else at Bethel Presbyterian, that by the same logic that complicated the sale of dogs they ought not to have whipped cream on their Jell-O, though any Orthodox Jew could have told them that. The Bible as rule book, in order to work at all, very much needs Mishnah and Talmuds and Responsa, or some hard-to-imagine Protestant equivalent. Pretty much the same is true of the Bible as treasury of obligatory beliefs. What is the biblical doctrine of marriage? (There is none, so far as I can see.) What does the Bible teach about homosexuality? (In its plain sense, absolutely nothing, because "homosexuality" is the invention of a peculiarly modern construction of sexuality unknown to anybody in antiquity, including the biblical writers.)[15]

Yet the rule-book advocates have on their side the fact that, when you consider the genres of the biblical texts, a lot of it sounds quite decidedly rulelike. Of course, there are a number of other genres as well: there are proverbs and riddles, wisdom sayings of all sorts, fables and short stories, poems and hymns, bits of liturgy and prayers, and a whole bunch of letters, some of which are really pamphlets in letter form, and some things hard to classify. In other words, to construe the plain sense of Scripture as narrative, one has to leave out a lot. We could, however, understand the Frei proposal in the following sense: from the entire Bible, it is possible to construct a kind of master narrative—as in fact the church has done in various ways through the centuries—and to make that narrative a touchstone by which our interpretation of all the parts has to be tested in various, constantly evolving ways.[16] That is something like what George Lindbeck means in talking about the intratextuality of the church.[17] What is worrisome about such a construal, however, is that it seems to entail a sectarian ecclesiology.[18] There are some good things about that in today's world: implicitly it renounces the triumphalism that has tacitly controlled our use of the master narrative, and which has so commonly devolved into our approval of the various forms of imperialism we have invented. But to be satisfied with the sectarian limits of our hermeneutics will mean in our present situation, I am afraid, to abandon the public square to that polarization between the Fundamentalists and the naive antireligionists that presently, *faute de mieux*, dominates all the mass media.

I think, on the whole, it is better to give up the notion of the *claritas scripturae* altogether, to stop telling people that the Bible clearly teaches anything, to admit to them that for the Bible to teach you anything you must be willing to submit to a rigorous discipline that entails, among other things, learning to be comfortable with ambiguity and a willingness to admit that there are things we do not know. The "radical" suggestion of Maurice Wiles, the Regius Professor of Theology at Oxford, is thus very appealing. He would renounce altogether the concept of the Bible as "binding authority" (the phrase is John Barton's), adopting instead the phrase "indispensable resource" to describe Scripture as authoritative. This would "make it easier for the church to acknowledge the varied nature of the stories to be found in the scriptural record," including the huge role of conflict within the church that produced some of the variety. "And having come to a fuller recognition of that, we will be the more ready to acknowledge the continuing presence of diversity and conflict in the later church, not simply as evidence of a sadly fallen later age but as a characteristic of how things are, for good as well as for ill." "For if the truth by which we are to live is not authoritatively given in the past but continually to be discovered in the present, such a process of discovery is bound to involve experimentation, with attendant error and conflict."[19]

Living with Obscurity

Let us then renounce the phrase, "The Bible clearly teaches . . . ," and every time we hear it, let us immediately be on our guard. Of course it is a convenient shorthand to personify the Bible as agent, in this case, as teacher. Saint Paul did something like that, when he quoted a text in Romans 10:6 with the introduction, "The righteousness that comes from faith says. . . ." But let us remember that when Paul said that, he then proceeded to give that text a meaning that was outrageously different from its contextual, grammatical plain sense. In our situation, when people say, "The Bible clearly teaches," instead of, say, "We can learn from the Bible if we stand within a certain community's tradition," or "We can find these ideas in Scripture if we construe Scripture in such and such a way," when they make the Bible the agent of their assertions, they are really masking the locus of the authority they are claiming.

It is better to confess obscurity. To be sure, part of the obscurity is the result of the fact that we are sinners, all of us, as Calvin and Luther said. But part of it is the result of the fact that "we know only in part, and we prophesy only in part; but when the complete comes, the partial will come to an end" (1 Cor. 13:9f.). As Hans Frei has said, "Let us assume that the notion of a right interpretation of the Bible is itself not meaningless, but it is eschatological."[20] He was thinking, I suppose, of what Paul said a few verses after the ones I just quoted: "For now we see through a glass darkly"—or in more contemporary English, "Now we see puzzling reflections in a mirror, but then we will see face to face. Now I know only in part; then I will know fully as I have been fully known" (v. 12, my translation). And then he adds, you will recall, that the thing that endures above all is love. That might be worth remembering amidst all our hermeneutical conundrums.

One last word. What has all this to do with Jesus, the ostensible subject of this book? Well, for one thing, this: New Testament writers celebrate Jesus as the fulfillment of Scripture. Yet we have seen that in order to see the events of the Jesus story as fulfilling Scripture, then the literal sense of Scripture, however construed, had often to be stood on its head. That was the reason for the vast interpretive drive of the first followers of Jesus, as we saw in chapter 3. The apostle Paul, as we saw in chapter 4, knew that better than anybody. For him to give up the clear meaning that Scripture had held for him was like having to die and to live again as if a new person were living in him. That's why he knew that the knowledge that counts comes only at the end, that the knowledge by which we struggle to live in the present is *en ainigmati*, like the puzzling reflections in a mirror.

Timothy Radcliffe, Scripture scholar and former Master of the Dominican Order, has understood the implications of this quite clearly. He sums up what he has learned about studying scriptural texts: "You cannot march in and claim their meaning with the aid of some grand theory. Study is much more like sneaking up on the meaning of the text, trying this approach and then another, inching one's way towards understanding." And the prayer of people who teach and study in universities, he goes on, should echo Blake: "May God us keep / From Single vision / And

Newton's sleep."[21] So, Radcliffe says, universities must, as their first duty, be "places of resistance to the imperialism of the single vision." And positively, they must be "places where we learn to talk to strangers."[22] What it might mean in the twenty-first century to talk to strangers about Jesus is the question of our final chapter.

Chapter Six

Is Jesus the Last Word?

It may be apparent by now that the approach to questions about Jesus' identity advocated here conflicts with one of the more cherished and ancient convictions of the church. That is the conviction that the revelation in Jesus is both final and complete, that Jesus is both the last word and the sufficient word about God's relation to humanity and humanity's hope for authentic existence. The Letter to the Hebrews sums it up, in words that have often served as a motto for the believer: "Jesus Christ is the same yesterday and today and forever" (Heb. 13:8). That claim may owe something to the popular Platonism of the author's day, which pitted the reality of the eternal against the shadowy realm of becoming, but it's right there in the Bible, and it's clear enough. And the statement stands directly counter to that understanding of identity proposed in chapter 2, which sees all human identity, including the identity of Jesus, as a continuous process of social transactions.

The motto from Hebrews also renders impossible any understanding of the Christian revelation that depends centrally on narrative, like the postliberal hermeneutic advocated by Hans Frei and his students, which I have adopted in part despite some reservations about it. For a story about a character who is the same yesterday and today and forever is going to be pretty boring. In fact, such a narrative arguably can have no plot. And a narrative without a plot is not merely boring; it is no narrative at all. Yet the Letter to the Hebrews itself depends quite centrally on narrative. In very imaginative fashion, it embodies that interpretive process that I called attention to in chapter 3. To revive the flagging enthusiasm of second-generation believers, it retells Jesus' story in a breathtakingly expansive way, set spatially in heaven and in earth, and temporally embracing the whole sweep of creation's history and destiny. Accordingly, we ought to forgive the author's overexuberance expressed in the quasi-Platonic sentiment, and pay attention rather to his method, which illustrates precisely that ongoing process of interaction between Jesus and his followers by which it becomes slowly clear who he is.

The church has always been torn between the desire to pin down its teaching about Jesus once and for all, in a system of static dogmas, and the acknowledgment that the story of God's engagement with the created world is dynamic and still open to God's perhaps surprising future. It will be apparent by now that I come down squarely on the latter side. There are, however, some dangers in this emphasis on the open-endedness of the story. Some of us are old enough to remember certain catastrophic applications of a doctrine of "progressive revelation" that was very popular with modernists at the turn of the twentieth century. It has been only three quarters of a century now since a great many "liberal" Christians in Germany saw in Adolf Hitler the latest revelation in God's ongoing plan.

The few courageous Christians who stood firm against this new gospel became the "Confessing Church" because they adopted as their bulwark against this pseudoprogressivism a quite "conservative" creed. Not every novelty announced in the name of Christ will turn out to be in tune with the dynamics of God's love. The open-endedness of God's story and the progressivism of modern industrial society are two different things altogether.

Our question is really twofold. First, is Jesus the last word? That is, is that identity of Jesus which has emerged through the process of interaction with his followers as described in chapter 2, and that process of interpretation illustrated in chapters 3 and 4—is that God's ultimate communication with God's creatures? Second, has the last word about Jesus already been spoken? My answer to the second part of the question is categorically no. The first half I find more difficult, for reasons I try to indicate in this chapter.

Let us begin by asking whether we can find a more helpful way of putting the question. Again, as so often, I turn to Hans Frei. Frei has insisted that, for Christians, the story of Jesus is unsurpassable. There is not, nor will there be, any story that can take its place. To take any other story as providing the master narrative within which our own life narratives must take their places would mean, quite simply, not to be Christians any longer. The story of Jesus, then, is for Christians unsurpassable.[1] But we must remember that Frei also said that if there is a right interpretation of the Bible, it can only be eschatological.[2] Frei would surely say the same about our understanding of who Jesus was, is, and will be. Of what kind of story can we say that it is unsurpassable, if we do not know quite how it will turn out so long as the present world endures?

Learning to Talk to Strangers

Father Timothy Radcliffe, O.P., has said that one of the primary jobs of people in universities—and by extension a desired vocation for the rest of us as well, especially for Christians—is to "resist the imperialism of the single vision" by learning "to talk to strangers."[3] I do not think there has been a moment in my lifetime when the threat of "the imperialism of the single vision" has been more dangerous than it is today. Nor has it ever perhaps in human history been more important to learn how to talk and listen to strangers. In the last century we have mastered the technology of killing strangers. And we have also mastered the psychological rule that it is easier to kill them so long as we are careful to keep them strangers. By now it is painfully obvious that this combination produces only a downward spiral of destruction and hatred. Security purchased by the psychological technique of dehumanizing the stranger; security purchased by the technology of murder, whether the expensive technology of guided missles or the cheap technology of suicide bombs, is no security at all. It brings no closure, and it brings no peace. In this situation learning to talk to strangers is no longer just a nice thing to do. It is a matter of survival.

For Christians the imperative of talking to strangers is especially strong and especially complicated. It has a history, which has been very powerful in its effects. But this history has had some quite troubling side-effects. This is a topic so vast we can barely scratch the surface in the present essay, but it requires our concentrated attention. Everyone can see that, in today's world, differences between religions are one of the primary ways in which estrangement of people from one another is formed and focused—whether or not such differences are the underlying cause of the estrangement. So when Father Timothy says that we must learn to talk to strangers, by strangers he means especially the whole non-Christian world. The strangers to whom we must learn to talk and to listen include both that majority who hold to other religious persuasions and live within narratives quite different from our story of Jesus and that growing number of people who are skeptical if not hostile toward all religious claims and all stories of transcendence.

From the very first followers of Jesus down to our own times, Christians have shown the most extraordinary zeal and the most astonishing ingenuity in talking to strangers of all kinds. Think of the physical energy, of the endurance of hardships, of the courage to face unfriendly climates, alien customs, perils of travel, all kinds of hostility. Think of the intellectual exertions in the endless work of translation, not only into different languages, but into different styles of philosophy, different modes of thinking, different cultures. The history of Christian missions comprises the most varied stories of adventure and fortitude, and many aspects of these stories remain marvelous to remember. And yet . . . the continuation of that history in our century becomes deeply problematical.

Why do we talk to strangers? The traditional answer has been, we talk to them only in order to convert them. Never mind that many missionaries discovered or knew from the start that conversion was not necessarily the point, nor the measure of success, of their efforts. The drive to engage those others has always been explicitly the drive to convert, and it is hard to refute the impression of so many of those others that by conversion we meant trying to make them as much as possible like ourselves. It is not just that in our post-Christian age many of us are uncomfortable with that program to convert the world, which we find unsophisticated and not very polite. There are also deeper problems with the conversionist program.

The first problem is pragmatic: "the conversion of the world in our generation" (the motto of the Student Volunteer Movement in the early twentieth century, which we now find so incredibly naive) is not going to happen. And one of the reasons it is not going to happen is the conviction of a great many of the world's peoples that Christian missions have served repeatedly as either the advance guard or the camp follower of Western imperialism—sometimes overtly, more often covertly or unconsciously. That suspicion is answered by our bad conscience as we acknowledge that indeed Christian missions have too often been complicit in colonialism in the past and, in the present, too often indistinguishable from the culture-destroying dimensions of the new globalization.

And the old and new forms of imperialism are not the only sins that have been hidden by the banner of Jesus' name. Think how many moral abominations the Bible has been called to support: The Crusades. Torture. Cruel and unusual punishments. American slavery. The oppression of women. Nationalist wars. Suppression of scientific inquiry. Antisemitism in all its guises. Racism. Bigotry of every description. Fear and loathing of every group that was different from our own. Given all the misery that has been caused by people who otherwise seemed good people and who said they were Christians and indeed *were* Christians, and who were acting in the name of Jesus and with what they were sure was the clear teaching of the Bible as their warrant—given those facts, it is really rather difficult to argue that the world would be a better place if everybody were a Christian.

On the contrary, it was a mistake to imagine that what God really wanted us to do was to make everyone else in the world like ourselves. Powerful as the conversionist drive has been in the history of Christendom, even acknowledging that the conversionist drive has accomplished much that is lasting and good, that is not the only way of reading the Bible or the Christian interpretive tradition. Nor is it the best way for our time. The argument throughout this book has been that the identity of Jesus is still open, that the transactive process by which identity is made is still going on. We are still learning who Jesus is, and we are still learning about the story of Creator and creation, the *logos* of God. We cannot write the last chapter of that Logos, because we see but dimly in mirrors, because we know only in part and we prophesy only in part. We do believe that, when the story is complete, it will include as one of its decisive turning points what Paul named the *logos tou staurou*, the story and trope and logic of the cross, but just how that fits into the whole story remains to be learned. And we will learn that only as we learn to listen and talk to strangers, to the other sheep of God who are not of this fold of ours, not of this Christian fold, not of this Western fold, not of this theistic fold.

What I am advocating is not a return to the naive humanism of, say, Lessing—although considering the blood shed by bigotry in the years since Lessing, his humanism does not look so bad, and his parable of the three rings is still affecting.[4] All the ways up the mountain are not equal, and they do not all lead automatically to the same reality. The peculiarities of the different traditions are not mere concealing husks that must be stripped from the truth that is the same for all. Reality is not something out there apart from the knowing. God is not the least common denominator of all our faiths nor the sum of the best in all our myths nor the essence that lies beneath all appearances and beyond all becoming. What is essential for the conversation among the religious traditions and between the religious and the irreligious traditions, the conversation we so desperately need to promote if we are to survive this century, is a resolutely honest acknowledgment of differences coupled with the determination to hear each other out and to press forward together, without masking our differences and without relinquishing what we each believe to be unsurpassable in our own traditions. The crucial question for Christians in our time—the crucial question for strong believers in every ongoing interpretive community—is how we can be faithful to those dimensions of our own lifeworld that our history has led us to deem irreplaceable, while at the same time opening our minds and our imaginations to the things we may need to discover—the things God may be trying to teach us, if you will—in those other traditions and lifeworlds that are now our unavoidable neighbors in this small planet. Perhaps surprisingly, the apostle Paul offers help.

The Surpassability of Jesus' Reign

We would certainly expect Paul, of all people, to agree with Hans Frei that the story of Jesus is "unsubstitutable." Because Paul believed that "the form of this world is passing away," and "the time has been cut short," and that in his own lifetime Jesus would come back in glory, it would surely be fair to think that he would take Jesus to be the last word. It is surprising, accordingly, to find him interrupting his proofs for the belief in the resurrection of the dead with the following account of Christ's *Parousia*, his royal Advent:

Then comes the end, when he hands over the kingdom to the God and Father, when God has abolished every rule and every authority and power. For he must reign until "[God] puts every enemy under his feet." As the last enemy, death, is abolished, for "[God] subordinated *all things* under his feet." Now when [Scripture] says, "all things" are subordinated, obviously that excludes the One who is subordinating "all things" to him. And when God subordinates all things to him, then the Son himself will be subordinated to the One who subordinated all things to him, in order for God to be all in all. (1 Cor.15:24–28, my translation)

That paragraph certainly makes it sound as if, for Paul, at least one part of the Jesus story, the story of his eventual triumph over all powers and his reign in glory, was not only surpassable, it would be surpassed in God's time. It is surprising how little is said about these verses in most commentaries. Or perhaps it is not surprising, given the fact that "Subordinationism" became a heresy in the ancient christological controversies, and so did Origen's notion of the return of all things to the beginning. Whatever the reason, the ancient commentaries talk of these verses only to explain that Paul did *not* mean either of those heretical notions, and most modern commentators say almost nothing about them, except to suggest that Paul was absentmindedly following some apocalyptic timetable or other to which we do not have to pay any attention.

John Chrysostom, however, as Margaret Mitchell pointed out several years ago, did take the passage seriously, and took it to be obviously part of Paul's rhetorical strategy in this whole letter, to combat the factionalism and status-conscious ambition that were tearing the

Corinthian house churches apart.[5] When all of the enemies lie at his feet, says Chrysostom, the Son, far from rebelling against the One who begot him, is at pains to demonstrate his concord, his *homonoia*. Chrysostom is right. Paul describes the ultimate submission of Christ's kingship to God as the supreme example of the sacrifice of one's own power and advantage for the sake of general concord. That is the same rhetorical use that Paul makes of his own story, especially in chapter 9, but in various ways throughout this letter. So once again we have that analogical working out of Jesus' story and the apostle's story in Paul's appeal for the moral formation of the communities he has founded. They ought to be imitators of him as he is of Christ, by letting the paradoxical power of God revealed in the Logos of the cross shape their form of life, rather than the competition for power and honor that pervades the world around them. And, by the way, Paul arrives at this remarkable scenario of Jesus' humble condescension by that kind of creative reinterpretation (and even rewriting) of biblical texts described above in chapter 3, and of which, in chapter 4, we found Paul to be a past master. Here Paul sets up a tension between the biblical text—in this instance the "twin" texts of Psalm 109:1 and 8:7 in the Septuagint—the story of Jesus that Paul had received as tradition and reshaped out of his own experience, and the present calamitous situation of the house churches. Through that interactive tension Paul perceives the way in which the grand narrative must culminate.[6]

Paul's Eschatological Hermeneutic

We are not Paul, and in our present situation we had better be very careful about the limits of the *imitatio Pauli*. Nevertheless, we still have a lot to learn from the kind of interpretive strategy to which he was driven by the unique situation in which he found himself after, as he said, "God who had singled [him] out from [his] mother's womb chose to reveal God's son in [him] (Gal. 1:15f., my trans.). That revelation turned his life upside down—no, his language, as we discovered in reading the Letter to the Galatians in chapter 4 above, is even more extreme: that new thing that God had done *killed* Paul's old life. "For through the law I died to the law, so that I might live to God" (2:19). Crucified with the absurdity of the crucified Messiah, Paul had died to that law which had been, he tells the Galatians, his whole life up until then. He had died to that whole structure of obedience which, he was certain, God had personally decreed as the covenanted form of life which constituted God's people. When Paul wrote to the Galatians, he saw these new converts as ready to "enslave" themselves to "weak and impoverished elements" of the old world. Therefore, he deliberately emphasized the contrast between the old and the new, between the world of striving to make oneself acceptable to God by means of one's keeping the rules of Torah and the freedom belonging to the new creation which the faithfulness of the Son of God had made. A reader of that letter could easily suppose that Paul was setting Christ against Torah, faith against law, even "Judaism" against "Christianity." In one aside, Paul emphatically denies that "the Torah is against the promises" (3:21, my trans.), but that seems a rather weak disclaimer in view of the vehemence of his main argument.

There was a hidden problem in this radically new appropriation of the Scriptures and traditions of Israel. The central question was this: Does God change his mind? Does he at one moment tell us that, in order to be his people, all our males must be circumcised, and we all must keep every rule that can be deduced from the Torah, and anyone who is crucified is a curse of God—and then at another moment does this same God tell us that his own Son the Messiah was crucified and that even Gentiles who are drawn to this crucified Messiah will be welcomed as God's people without being circumcised?

In his argument against the new apostles in Galatia, Paul emphasizes the radicality of his claim and, understandably, not that terrible underlying problem. But by the time he wrote the longest of his letters, the one to the congregations that were not his own in Rome, this problem had become the center of his concern. This was not merely a problem of Paul's conscience. It was not just an unresolved issue of his own biography. It is not just a question for those interpreters who wonder why Paul is not consistent. It is rather a question about God. It is not Paul's consistency that is at question, but God's. If God's action in Christ was as radical as Paul claims, then (as Paul Meyer puts it), "what . . . becomes of God's faithfulness, that very reliability on which human trust, beginning with Abraham's, can alone depend?"[7] The question is, can you trust a God who is unpredictable? The answer Paul gives in the Letter to the Romans is that we can trust God precisely *because* God is unpredictable. We can trust God because God's intention for the creation is too vast for us to comprehend, wonderful beyond our petty notions of consistency. We can trust God because God's love welcomes those whom our fears would exclude, embraces those whom our predictions would assume to be God's enemies and ours. And Paul answers the question by not answering it. Instead he constructs a story that is itself full of surprises. In this story the Gentiles are astonished because the God of Israel has brought good news to them. The unrighteous are astonished to find God declaring them righteous. The righteous are astonished that God would welcome the unrighteous. The enemies of God are astonished by God's amnesty. The people of God are astonished to find themselves unmasked as themselves God's enemies insofar as they resist this unpredictable and unseemly expansion of God's love. The Jews are astonished by the absurd story of the crucified Messiah, and they are scandalized by the notion that this bunch of goys are now God's people. The Gentiles are astonished that Paul still thinks the Jews are God's people and that the call and election of Israel are irrevocable—or, as we might as well translate, unsurpassable.[8]

Paul's rhetorical method in this letter matches the astonishing story he is telling, for the reader is surprised at every turn by the twists and paradoxes that Paul introduces and emphasizes. Not least are the surprises that Paul contrives by his outrageous way of interpreting Scripture. It is not just that he turns the plain sense of familiar verses upside down. He does it in such a way that anyone who knows the Bible at all will see what he is doing. As Richard Hays so lucidly explained, Paul sets his novel interpretation over against the plain sense of the text in such a way that they become like two strings plucked together to produce a strange, almost comic assonance, so that by the very contradictions a new tone is set ringing and a new song is sung.[9] Romans is a letter whose rhetoric gives the reader a lot of work to do. It places us as readers into that same perplexing situation in which the Jews and Gentiles of the congregations at Rome and Paul's congregations in the provinces find themselves. It is an anomalous situation in which there is no easy resolution, such as those the successors of Paul so often chose: In with the New, out with the Old. Once the Jews were God's people, now the Christians are. Christians are living out *Heilsgeschichte*, the history of God's salvation; Jews are living out *Unheilsgeschichte*, the history of God's curse. We are all too familiar with those solutions, which are not only expressed in other early Christian writings, but have overtly or tacitly controlled the relationship between Jews and Christians throughout most of Christian history. Paul does not allow any of them. He does not offer a resolution; only God can do that, and not until the End. Then it will be revealed that "God has locked up all people in disobedience, in order to have mercy on all" (Rom. 11:32, my trans.). The climax of Paul's argument is not a solution but a doxology:

> O the depth of the riches and wisdom and knowledge of God! How unsearchable are his judgments and how inscrutable his ways!
>
> "For who has known the mind of the Lord?
>   Or who has been his counselor?"
> Or who has given a gift to him,
>   to receive a gift in return?
>
> For from him and through him and to him are all things. To him be the glory forever. Amen. (11:33–36)

Paul is not being evasive. He is rather expressing by the very form of his rhetoric that paradoxicality of the story of God that always points beyond the fragile and distorting mirrors in which we see its truth enigmatically reflected. And this is not, as we say, "just rhetoric." It is rhetoric that is designed to do what all Paul's letters try to do: to form a community that will embody the shape of that partially and enigmatically perceived story in the form of their life together. So the climax of the story about the Jews and the Gentiles as God's peculiar people, which occupies chapters 9–11 of Romans but has been introduced at the very beginning, is set into Paul's practical admonitions about the way in which people of quite different everyday ways of living out their faith, some strong and some weak, ought to deal with one another—and this issue has also been in Paul's view from the beginning of the letter. He was new to Rome, but he certainly knew a lot about the kind of conflict that he here imagines could happen there, because he had seen it first hand in Corinth. Here, more carefully and with greater literary precision than in the letter to Corinth (1 Cor. 8–10), he lays out the concerns of each side—and what each side is doing to its opponents. And he sums up, as you may remember, with these words: "Welcome one another, therefore, just as Christ has welcomed you, for the glory of God" (Rom. 15:7).

Paul's eschatological hermeneutic does not just consist in retelling the old, old story, nor even in transforming the old, old story by the new, new story, though he does both things. At the center of Paul's concern is his labor to give birth, as he rather dramatically puts it in the Letter to Galatians, to a community that will be conformed to that story, whose form of life will be analogous to that paradoxical story of life in death, of power in weakness, of joy in suffering, of judgment and waiting, of striving and receiving, a community in which "Christ will be formed" (Gal. 4:19, my trans.). In Paul's version of this story, the event of the crucified Messiah radically transforms the story of Israel—but it does not supplant it. The calling and election of Israel are still irrevocable, the history of God and Israel unsurpassable. So, also, the story of Jesus, the Logos of the cross, is unsurpassable, even though, at the end, as Son he will hand over the kingdom to God.

The Story of Jesus in the Postmodern World

When we talk, as we must, to the strangers who have become our necessary neighbors in this newly small planet, what shall we say about Jesus? To our Muslim neighbors, and our Buddhist neighbors, to our atheist neighbors, and our pragmatist neighbors, what shall we say? We will not say, "It doesn't matter what you believe as long as you're sincere," because it does matter deeply, and they know that and we know that. We will not say, "Let's just not talk about religion, because religion is a private matter," because religion that means anything at all is not private but quite social and public, and it forms communities—for good and for ill. We will not say, "Let's just talk about the things we agree on, and ignore the differences," because the differences are not only important, they are the very points of tension where we have most to learn from one another.

And when I talk with my Muslim neighbor, and he tells me of the story of Issa as the Qur'an tells it, the Issa who is a great but not the last prophet, the Issa who could not have suffered as the Gospels say, it is not the case that the only way we can go on being neighbors who learn from each other is if I accept that story or he accepts the Gospel story. It is certainly not the case that we have to decide not to talk about those conflicting stories. But we can talk to each other about what the consequences are when communities try to shape themselves in accord with those differing stories, and the other stories of our frequently conflicting traditions. And we will look for intersections and we will look for ways in which each of us can learn from those things which one of us cannot give up, because that part of the story is unsurpassable, and the other cannot accept, because that would mean giving up something central to a way of life that had been precious for a long time. And something like that extended and open-ended conversation will have to take place with each of those other strange and sometimes prickly neighbors.

This delicate and dangerous conversation is necessary for Christians because, if Paul is right, then surely we have not seen the last surprise in God's plan to bring the unruly human denizens of creation into some kind of habits of justice and peace and love. If Paul is right, the God of the Bible will astonish the people who claim to be God's over and over again, but God will not betray those who put their confidence in God's story. The ultimate story, which we will learn only when we know as we are known, will still include, in a way that is now unfathomable to us, that paradoxical *logos tou staurou*, that story and trope and logic of the cross and resurrection of Jesus, but it will include much else as well, far beyond our imagining.

So how ought we to imagine the End of Days—the last chapter of the Jesus story, the ultimate shape of Jesus' identity? Shall we imagine Jesus standing in armor, his foot on the neck of the conquered infidel? Shall we imagine the Jesus of Michelangelo's Sistine ceiling, averting his gaze from the anguished hordes of the pagans and heretics and sinners who are being dragged off to hell? Or shall we imagine a Christ who smiles at the surprise of those sons of Abraham who come from east and west to join him in the kingdom that now is to be handed over to the one inscrutable God, who cannot imagine that they are really here? Can you picture the Son of the Human who, at the last judgment when he sits on his throne, surprises the sheep on his right as much as the goats on the left: "Lord, when did we see you . . . ?"

When we sing, "Jesus shall reign where'er the sun / does its successive journeys run," let us remember Justin

Martyr's peculiar reading of Psalm 95 LXX, "The Lord reigned from the tree" (1 Apol. 41:4). That is, the victory of the Son of God is not that of the triumphalist church's dreams, but the victory that reveals the heart of the loving, inscrutable, ironic God. The story that centers on that paradoxical reign and culminates when the last enemy, Death, is vanquished and the Son hands the whole thing over—let us remember that that story is called "Good News." It is not a rule book. It is not a set of doctrines. It is above all not a ransom note. It is a love letter.

Notes

Preface

1. The Dahl lecture has been published as "Inventing the Christ: Multicultural Process and Poetry Among the First Christians," *Studia Theologica* 58 (2004): 77–96.

Chapter 1

1. Augustine, *Confessions* 1.1.1, my translation.
2. The "Gentle Jesus" line is from a hymn originally written in 1742 by Charles Wesley. The imposing mosaic of Jesus with hands uplifted in blessing (or, as fans believe, declaring a touchdown) adorns the wall of the Hesburgh Library at the University of Notre Dame, overlooking the stadium; its common nickname serves as a fitting title for R. Laurence Moore's *Touchdown Jesus: The Mixing of Sacred and Secular in American History* (Louisville, KY: Westminster John Knox Press, 2003). For the incredible success of Sallman's drawing, see *Icons of American Protestantism: The Art of Warner Sallman*, ed. David Morgan (New Haven, CT: Yale University Press, 1996). Apparently its popularity is no longer limited to Protestants; an online Catholic source offers a color print, in an "antique gold frame," for $115, along with "an outstanding selection of Catholic Books and Gifts, Bibles, Catechisms, Bible Studies, Rosaries, Crosses, Crucifixes, Miraculous Medals, Statues, Catholic Jewelry, Art, Videos, and DVDs." Stephen R. Prothero, *American Jesus: How the Son of God Became a National Icon* (New York: Farrar, Straus and Giroux, 2003), 200–228, surveys some of the attempts to find a black Jesus, and describes womanist theology on 207–8, 223–26. *The Man Nobody Knows* was a bestseller from its publication in 1925 by Bruce Barton, one of the inventors of modern advertising and one of the founders of the immensely successful firm Batten, Barton, Durstine, and Osborne; see Richard Wightman Fox, *Jesus in*

America: Personal Savior, Cultural Hero, National Obsession (San Francisco: HarperSanFrancisco, 2004), 318–23, and, on Jesus as social reformer, 283–94. Fox does not point out the parallel between Barton's notion of servanthood and the motto of Rotary International, coined by Arthur Sheldon and adopted at the Rotary convention of 1911 (see http://www.rotaryhistoryfellowship.org/leaders/sheldon/). In June 2001 this part of the motto was abandoned, only to be reinstated by the Board of Directors in November of the same year (see http://www.rotary.org/support/board/0111.html). Among the pioneers of feminist interpretation Elisabeth Schüssler Fiorenza stands out, with her *In Memory of Her: A Feminist Theological Reconstruction of Christian Origins* (New York: Crossroad, 1983) and (among many other publications) *But She Said: Feminist Practices of Biblical Interpretation* (Boston: Beacon Press, 1992).

3. Fox, *Jesus in America*, 395.

4. Edward Gibbon, *The Decline and Fall of the Roman Empire* (New York: The Modern Library, 1932), 1:690. He refers to the two Greek words, both adapted from the technical vocabulary of Platonism, *homoousios* and *homoiousios*, which became the watchwords of the "Catholics" and the "semi-Arians," respectively, in the arguments over the divine nature of Jesus.

5. A very readable brief account of the (Nicene-Constantinopolitan) Creed, its loss of authority under the stress of modernity, and its continuing significance for all catholic (with small or large C) Christians may be found in Luke Timothy Johnson, *The Creed: What Christians Believe and Why It Matters* (New York: Doubleday, 2003). On the controversy alluded to above, 129–32.

6. Gotthold Ephraim Lessing, "On the Proof of the Spirit and of Power," in *Lessing's Theological Writings*, selected and trans. Henry Chadwick, A Library of Modern Religious Thought (Stanford, CA: Stanford University Press, 1957), 53.

7. David Friedrich Strauss, *Das Leben Jesu, kritisch bearbeitet* (Tübingen: C. F. Osiander, 1835–36); David Friedrich Strauss, *Das Leben Jesu für das deutsche Volk* (Leipzig: F. A. Brockhaus, 1864); David Friedrich Strauss, *The Life of Jesus Critically Examined*, trans. George Eliot (London: Chapman Brothers, 1846); Ernest Renan, *Vie de Jésus* (Paris: Michel Lévy Frères, 1863); Ernest Renan, *The Life of Jesus*, trans. Charles E. Wilbour (New York: Carleton, 1864); Albert Schweitzer, *The Quest of the Historical Jesus*, ed. John Bow-

den, trans. W. Montgomery, J.R. Coates, Susan Cupitt, and John Bowden (London: SCM Press, 2000), from the German edition of 1913; its original German title, 1906, had been "From Reimarus to Wrede: A History of the Life-of-Jesus Investigation").

8. Louis Dupré, *Passage to Modernity: An Essay in the Hermeneutics of Nature and Culture* (New Haven, CT, and London: Yale University Press, 1993), 38.

9. Pseudo-Bonaventure, *Meditations on the Life of Christ: An Illustrated Manuscript of the Fourteenth Century*, ed. and trans. Isa Ragusa and Rosalie Green, Princeton Monographs in Art and Archaeology (Princeton, NJ: Princeton University Press, 1961), 44, quoted by Leo Steinberg, *The Sexuality of Christ in Renaissance Art and in Modern Oblivion* (New York: Pantheon, 1983), 57.

10. Steinberg, *Sexuality*, passim. Not surprisingly, Steinberg's claim to have discovered a new emphasis on Christ's sexuality by painters between 1260 and 1540 evoked a lively and often critical response from other art historians as well as some theologians. He responded to his critics with an extended defense of his position in a second edition of the book (Chicago: University of Chicago Press, 1996). Certainly not everyone will see what Steinberg saw in each of the thousand-odd examples on which he bases his argument, but the cumulative weight of the argument is not easy to refute. For an amusing review that tells as much about the reception of the book as about Steinberg's work, see Griselda Pollock, "Erudite, Intelligent, Revealing," *The Art Book* 5, no. 1 (January 1998): 10–11.

11. A particularly eloquent account of the developments I have so superficially sketched here is to be found in some of the essays included in Anthony Grafton, *Bring Out Your Dead: The Past as Revelation* (Cambridge, MA: Harvard University Press, 2001), further illuminated by the fine review of Grafton by Keith Thomas, "Heroes of History," *New York Review of Books* 50, no. 4 (13 March 2003): 38–40. On the rise of skepticism and Montaigne's role, see also Dupré, *Passage to Modernity*, 112-15, and Charles Taylor, *Sources of the Self: The Making of the Modern Identity* (Cambridge, MA: Harvard University Press, 1989), 177–84.

12. Dupré, *Passage to Modernity*, chap. 4.

13. For an elegant evocation of these currents of thought—and more—in eighteenth-century Britain, see "Rationalizing Religion" in Roy Porter, *The Creation of the Modern World: The Untold*

Story of the British Enlightenment (London and New York: Norton, 2001), 96–129. The whole book is pertinent to our topic. The loss of transcendence and the consequent crisis in modern theology is the principal theme of Dupré's *Passage to Modernity*.

14. John Lewis Gaddis, *The Landscape of History: How Historians Map the Past* (New York: Oxford, 2002), 89 et passim.

15. The line, endlessly quoted, usually out of context, is from Franz Leopold von Ranke, who thus humbly contrasted the task he adopted with those grander presumptions of older historians: "People have attributed to history the task of judging the past, of instructing our contemporaries for the benefit of future years—but the present attempt presumes no such high ambition; it wants only to show how it really was." [Man hat der Historie das Amt, die Vergangenheit zu richten, die Mitwelt zum Nutzen zukünftiger Jahre zu belehren, beigemessen: so hoher Aemter unterwindet sich gegenwärtiger Versuch nicht: er will blos zeigen, wie es eigentlich gewesen.] (*Sämtliche Werke*, vol. 33/34 [Leipzig: Duncker & Humblot, 1885], p. 7, my translation).

16. "Against positivism, which halts at phenomena—'There are only *facts*'—I would say: No, facts is precisely what there is not, only interpretations" (Friedrich Nietzsche, *The Will to Power*, ed. Walter Kaufmann, trans. Walter Kaufmann and R. J. Hollingdale [New York: Random House, 1968], 267).

17. Dupré, *Passage to Modernity*, 115; cf. Taylor, *Sources of the Self*, 143–58; Jeffrey Stout, *The Flight from Authority: Religion, Morality, and the Quest for Autonomy* (Notre Dame, IN; London: University of Notre Dame Press, 1981), 25–61.

18. Taylor, *Sources of the Self*, 144; italics original.

19. Ibid., 175–76.

20. Developments in the philosophy of science under the impact of the new physics have been so rapid it is hard for a nonspecialist to single out the best place to begin. Among the most influential have been Thomas S. Kuhn, *The Structure of Scientific Revolutions*, vol. 2, number 2 of *Foundations of the Unity of Science*, International Encyclopedia of Unified Science, 2nd ed. (Chicago: University of Chicago Press, 1967), and Richard Rorty, *Philosophy and the Mirror of Nature* (Princeton, NJ: Princeton University Press, 1979). Among the many responses to Rorty, Kai Nielsen, *After the Demise of the Tradition: Rorty, Critical Theory, and the Fate of Philosophy* (Boulder, CO: Westview Press, 1991), is useful and provocative.

21. John Patrick, *The Teahouse of the August Moon* (New York: Putnam, 1954), Act 1, Scene 1, p. 8.
22. Paul Ricoeur, *Freud and Philosophy: An Essay on Interpretation*, trans. Denis Savage (New Haven, CT: Yale University Press, 1970), 33–36.
23. One of the most helpful reviews of these developments is Garrett Green, *Theology, Hermeneutics, and Imagination: The Crisis of Interpretation at the End of Modernity* (Cambridge and New York: Cambridge University Press, 2000). Green shows that the master thinker behind "Ricoeur's triumvirate," Freud, Nietzsche, and Marx, was Feuerbach, and what was most important for Feuerbach was that for him the object of suspicion was *the imagination*. Imagination produced fiction; scientific inquiry produced fact (13–14). But today, in the "twilight of modernity," it becomes apparent that this dichotomy between reality and imagination is crumbling (205); indeed, "Imagination now becomes the unavoidable means of apprehending 'reality,' though there is, of course, no guarantee that it will succeed" (14).

Chapter 2

1. Schweitzer, *The Quest of the Historical Jesus*, 478.
2. Albert Schweitzer, *Das Messianitäts- und Leidensgeheimnis: eine Skizze des Lebens Jesu* (Tübingen: J. C. B. Mohr [P. Siebeck], 1956; originally pub. 1901); English: Albert Schweitzer, *The Mystery of the Kingdom of God: The Secret of Jesus' Messiahship and Passion*, trans. Walter Lowrie (New York: Schocken, 1964; originally pub. 1914).
3. Søren Kierkegaard, *Attack Upon "Christendom" 1854–1855*, trans. and introd. Walter Lowrie (Princeton, NJ: Princeton University Press, 1968).
4. Karl Barth, *Church Dogmatics*, trans. and ed. Geoffrey William Bromiley and Thomas Forsyth Torrance (Edinburgh: T. & T. Clark, 1957).
5. Rudolf Bultmann, *Jesus and the Word*, trans. Louise Pettibone Smith and Erminie Huntress Lantero (New York: Scribner's, 1958), 9.
6. Hans W. Frei, *The Eclipse of Biblical Narrative: A Study in Eighteenth- and Nineteenth-Century Hermeneutics* (New Haven, CT: Yale University Press, 1974); Hans W. Frei, *The Identity of Jesus Christ, the Hermeneutical Bases of Dogmatic Theology* (1967; repr. Philadelphia: Fortress Press, 1975).

7. Ernst Käsemann, "Das Problem des historischen Jesus," in *Exegetische Versuche und Besinnungen* (Göttingen: Vandenhoeck & Ruprecht, 1964), 1:187–214; first published in 1954; English: Ernst Käsemann, "The Problem of the Historical Jesus," in *Essays on New Testament Themes*, trans. W. J. Montague (London: SCM, 1964), 15–47. Bultmann's response is found in his "The Primitive Christian Kerygma and the Historical Jesus," in *The Historical Jesus and the Kerygmatic Christ: Essays on the New Quest of the Historical Jesus*, trans. and ed. Carl E. Braaten and Roy A. Harrisville (New York and Nashville: Abingdon, 1964), 15–42.

8. James M. Robinson, *A New Quest of the Historical Jesus*, Studies in Biblical Theology 25 (London: SCM Press, 1959).

9. Rudolf Bultmann, *Jesus Christ and Mythology* (New York: Scribner's, 1958), 55.

10. Jeffrey Stout, *The Flight from Authority: Religion, Morality, and the Quest for Autonomy* (Notre Dame, IN, and London: University of Notre Dame Press, 1981).

11. Hans W. Frei, *The Eclipse of Biblical Narrative: A Study in Eighteenth- and Nineteenth-Century Hermeneutics* (New Haven, CT: Yale University Press, 1974).

12. George A. Lindbeck, *The Nature of Doctrine: Religion and Theology in a Post-Liberal Age* (Philadelphia: Westminster Press, 1984), 16.

13. Schweitzer, *The Quest of the Historical Jesus*, 487.

14. Phil. 2:5–11, my translation.

15. It is estimated that about thirty thousand texts have been published to date; countless others, many quite small and fragmentary and difficult to decipher, still languish in collections all over the world. For a brief overview, see Herwig Maehler, "Papyrology," in *The Oxford Classical Dictionary* (Oxford and New York: Oxford University Press, 1996), 1109–11.

16. For brief accounts of the history of modern textual criticism, see Bruce Manning Metzger, *The Text of the New Testament: Its Transmission, Corruption, and Restoration* (New York: Oxford University Press, 1992), and Kurt Aland and Barbara Aland, *The Text of the New Testament: An Introduction to the Critical Editions and to the Theory and Practice of Modern Textual Criticism*, trans. Erroll F. Rhodes (Grand Rapids: W. B. Eerdmans, 1989).

17. Some may still remember the furor that surrounded the publication of the Revised Standard Version in 1948. When the RSV Old Testament was completed and published in 1952 in a red buckram

binding, many conservatives denounced it as "the Red Bible." Many evangelicals, however, were enthusiastic supporters of both the advances in textual criticism and in the efforts to bring translations up to date.

18. The insistence on Semitic undertones of NT Greek was already an important principle for the great eighteenth-century philologian, Johann August Ernesti, on whom see William Baird, *History of New Testament Research* (Minneapolis: Fortress Press, 1992–2003), 1:108–14. To that end the Cambridge scholar John Lightfoot had, even earlier, begun the careful comparison of NT texts with rabbinic literature—an enterprise that was pursued with great zeal in the late nineteenth and early twentieth centuries by Gustav Dalman and his students, including Joachim Jeremias. Gerhard Kittel took up this inquiry in a peculiar and ultimately self-destructive fashion, culminating in the famous but very often misleading publication, mostly after his death, Gerhard Kittel, Otto Bauernfeind, and Gerhard Friedrich, *Theological Dictionary of the New Testament*, ed. and trans. Geoffrey William Bromiley (Grand Rapids: Eerdmans, 1964–76). On this see Wayne A. Meeks, "A Nazi New Testament Professor Reads His Bible: The Strange Case of Gerhard Kittel," in *The Idea of Biblical Interpretation: Essays in Honor of James L. Kugel*, ed. Hindy Najman and Judith H. Newman (Leiden and Boston: Brill, 2004), 513–44, and, on the semantic fallacies of the whole business, James Barr, *The Semantics of Biblical Language* (Oxford: Oxford University Press, 1961).

19. Deissmann's insights were widely disseminated in two books, Adolf Deissmann, *Bible Studies: Contributions, Chiefly from Papyri and Inscriptions, to the History of the Language, the Literature, and the Religion of Hellenistic Judaism and Primitive Christianity*, trans. A. J. Grieve (Edinburgh: T. & T.Clark, 1901; first published in German in 1895), and *Light from the Ancient East: The New Testament Illustrated by Recently Discovered Texts of the Graeco-Roman World*, trans. Lionel R. M. Strachan (London: Hodder & Stoughton, 1910; first German edition 1908). For a good short account of Deissmann's work, see Werner Georg Kümmel, *The New Testament: The History of the Investigation of Its Problems*, trans. S. McLean Gilmour and Howard C. Kee (Nashville: Abingdon Press, 1972), 218–19. The importance of papyri and inscriptions for linguistic and sociohistorical study of antiquity, including early Judaism and Christianity, has only grown since Deissmann's era. See, for example, the useful

surveys of evidence produced by a growing number of scholars working with a team at Macquarie University in Australia, *New Documents Illustrating Early Christianity*, ed. G. H. R. Horsley (vols. 1–5) and S. R. Llewelyn (vols. 6–) (North Ryde, N.S.W.: Ancient History Documentary Research Centre, Macquarie University, 1981–). Their studies and others' have further refined the notion of the *koinē*, distinguishing between chronological changes in usage—the *koinē* being assigned roughly to the period of the successors of Alexander the Great and later—and variations of register depending on social level and linguistic function: one can also speak of a "literary *koinē*," for example, or compare the style of some parts of the NT with that of handbooks and technical manuals. Some of these issues are dealt with briefly in vol. 6 of *New Documents*, entitled *Linguistic Essays* (1989).

20. Quoted in Kümmel, *The New Testament* (see previous note), 219. Deissmann also pioneered in a revisionary reading of Paul's letters as not "epistles"—written by literati with an eye to publication—but "real" letters for specific occasions and purposes, and he tried to set Paul and his congregations, too, into a more realistic social context: Adolf Deissmann, *Paul: A Study in Social and Religious History*, trans. William E. Wilson (New York: Harper & Row, 1957; first German edition, 1911; first English translation, by L. R. M. Strachan, 1912).

21. The prime example of this exaggeration was the work of Morton Smith, the distinguished historian of Columbia University, *Jesus the Magician* (San Francisco: Harper & Row, 1978), a work of extraordinary learning and wit, but also of serious distortions. The exploration of the magical papyri has produced quite a vast literature, including accessible collections of the spells in translation, like Hans Dieter Betz, ed., *The Greek Magical Papyri in Translation, Including the Demotic Spells* (Chicago and London: University of Chicago Press, 1986), and John G. Gager, ed. and trans., *Curse Tablets and Binding Spells from the Ancient World* (New York and Oxford: Oxford University Press, 1992). Among the numerous inquiries into the implications of magical practice and beliefs for understanding early Christianity, two particularly helpful examples are Susan R. Garrett, *The Demise of the Devil: Magic and the Demonic in Luke's Writings* (Minneapolis: Fortress Press, 1989), and Hans-Josef Klauck, *Magic and Paganism in Early Christianity: The World of the Acts of the Apostles*, trans. Brian McNeil (Edinburgh: T. & T.

Clark, 2000). On the broader question of "superstition" as the concept was used by ancient writers, altogether different from the prevailing usage in modernism, see the pioneering work by Dale B. Martin, *Inventing Superstition: From the Hippocratics to the Christians* (Cambridge, MA, and London: Harvard University Press, 2004).

22. The point of view of Karl Kautsky, *Foundations of Christianity: A Study in Christian Origins* (New York: Monthly Review Press, 1972; originally published, 1925).

23. On the problems of the "original text" and the importance of seeing some later changes as not just "errors" but reflections of different generations' understanding of the texts, see Bart D. Ehrman, "Text and Tradition: The Role of New Testament Manuscripts in Early Christian Studies. The Kenneth W. Clark Lectures, Duke Divinity School, 1997," *TC: A Journal of Biblical Textual Criticism* [http://purl.Org/TC] 5 (2000) [an electronic journal].

24. André Dupont-Sommer, *The Essene Writings from Qumran*, trans. Geza Vermes (Gloucester, MA: Peter Smith, 1973), 360.

25. B. E. Thiering, *The Gospels and Qumran: A New Hypothesis*, Australian and New Zealand Studies in Theology and Religion (Sydney: Theological Explorations, 1981).

26. Of the flood of publications, the following will give a reliable overview: James C. VanderKam and Peter W. Flint, *The Meaning of the Dead Sea Scrolls: Their Significance for Understanding the Bible, Judaism, Jesus, and Christianity* (San Francisco: HarperSanFrancisco, 2002); *The Community of the Renewed Covenant: The Notre Dame Symposium on the Dead Sea Scrolls*, ed. Eugene Charles Ulrich and James C. VanderKam, Christianity and Judaism in Antiquity (Notre Dame, IN: University of Notre Dame Press, 1994); Florentino García Martínez and Julio Trebolle Barrera, *The People of the Dead Sea Scrolls: Their Writings, Beliefs, and Practices* (Leiden: E. J. Brill, 1995). For a fascinating firsthand account of the earliest discoveries, see John C. Trever, *The Dead Sea Scrolls: A Personal Account*, rev. ed. (Grand Rapids: Eerdmans, 1977).

27. Gospel of Thomas, sayings 77 and 114, and Gospel of Philip 48 (63:30–64:5), as trans. by Bentley Layton, trans. and ed., *The Gnostic Scriptures: A New Translation with Annotations and Introductions* (Garden City, NY: Doubleday, 1987), 394, 114, 339. The brackets represent lacunae in the manuscript and some conjectural reconstructions of the missing words.

28. On the "Mandaean fever," as one scholar called it, see Werner Georg Kümmel, *The New Testament: The History of the Investigation of Its Problems*, trans. S. McLean Gilmour and Howard C. Kee (Nashville: Abingdon Press, 1972), 349–62; Bultmann's proposals were first enunciated in "Die Bedeutung der neuerschlossenen mandäischen und manichäischen Quellen für das Verständnis des Johannesevangeliums," *ZNW* 24 (1925): 100–146, and eventually incorporated into his rightly celebrated commentary: Rudolf Karl Bultmann, *The Gospel of John: A Commentary* (Oxford: Blackwell, 1971). For a critique, see Wayne A. Meeks, *The Prophet-King: Moses Traditions and the Johannine Christology*, Supplements to Novum Testamentum (Leiden: Brill, 1967).

29. *Die Pseudepigraphen des Alten Testaments*, vol. 2 of *Die Apokryphen und Pseudepigraphen des Alten Testaments*, ed. and trans. E. Kautzsch (Tübingen: Mohr, 1900); *Pseudepigrapha*, vol. 2 of *The Apocrypha and Pseudepigrapha of the Old Testament in English*, ed. R. H. Charles (Oxford: Clarendon, 1913); *The Old Testament Pseudepigrapha*, ed. James H. Charlesworth (Garden City, NY: Doubleday, 1983–1985). Research in the individual documents included in these collections continues, in many cases revising older views substantially. Especially important is a series of detailed investigations published in the series *Studia in veteris testamenti pseudepigrapha* (Leiden: Brill, 1970–); at this writing some eighteen volumes have been published.

30. See the symposium volume *Apocalypticism in the Mediterranean World and the Near East: Proceedings of the International Colloquium on Apocalypticism, Uppsala, August 12–17, 1979*, ed. David Hellholm (Tübingen: Mohr-Siebeck, 1983), esp. 329–637, "The Literary Genre of Apocalypses." The Colloquium adjourned without being able to agree on a definition of "apocalypse" or "apocalypticism."

31. Johannes Weiss, *Die Predigt Jesu vom Reiche Gottes* (Göttingen: Vandenhoeck & Ruprecht, 1892; English: *Jesus' Proclamation of the Kingdom of God*, Lives of Jesus Series [Philadelphia: Fortress Press, 1971]; Albert Schweitzer, *Das Messianitäts- und Leidensgeheimnis: eine Skizze des Lebens Jesu* (Tübingen: Mohr-Siebeck, 1956; first pub. 1901; English: *The Mystery of the Kingdom of God: The Secret of Jesus' Messiahship and Passion*, trans. Walter Lowrie [New York: Schocken, 1964; first pub. 1914]).

32. The banner of the Tübingen School's evolutionary revision of

early Christian history was first raised by F. C. Baur, "Die Christuspartei in der korinthischen Gemeinde, der Gegensatz des petrinischen und paulinischen Christenthums in der ältesten Kirche, der Apostel Petrus in Rom," *Tübinger Zeitschrift für Theologie* 4 (1831): 61–206. For a full account of the development see P. C. Hodgson, *The Formation of Historical Theology: A Study of Ferdinand Christian Baur*, Makers of Modern Theology (New York: Harper and Row, 1966). A searching challenge to the basis of Baur's construct and its continuing influence: C. C. Hill, *Hellenists and Hebrews: Reappraising Division within the Earliest Church* (Minneapolis: Augsburg Fortress, 1992).

33. Ferdinand Christian Baur, *The Church History of the First Three Centuries*, trans. Allan Menzies (London: Williams and Norgate, 1878), 1:58.

34. See J. Rüsen, *Begriffene Geschichte: Genesis und Begründung der Geschichtstheorie J. G. Droysens*, Sammlung Schöningh zur Geschichte und Gegenwart (Paderborn: Ferdinand Schöningh, 1969), esp. 28–37, 46–49, 133–41. Droysen's best-known work is *Geschichte des Hellenismus*, ed. E. Bayer (Basel: B. Schwabe, 1952–1953).

35. The classic statement of this thesis was by Wilhelm Heitmüller, "Zum Problem Paulus und Jesus," *Zeitschrift für die neutestamentliche Wissenschaft* 13 (1912): 320–37, trans. in part in Wayne A. Meeks, ed., *The Writings of St. Paul: A Norton Critical Edition* (New York: W. W. Norton, 1972), 308–19. The same scheme provides the intellectual framework for Rudolf Bultmann, *Theology of the New Testament*, trans. Kendrick Grobel (New York: Scribner's, 1951).

36. I have discussed the "Judaism-Hellenism" problem at greater length in Wayne A. Meeks, "Judaism, Hellenism, and the Birth of Christianity," in *Paul Beyond the Judaism/Hellenism Divide*, ed. Troels Engberg-Pedersen (Louisville, KY: Westminster John Knox Press, 2001), 17–28, from which several of the preceding paragraphs are taken.

37. I. M. Bakhtin, *Freudianism: A Marxist Critique*, ed. and trans. by Neal H. Brass (New York: Academic Press, 1976), 76f., quoted by Katerina Clark and Michael Holquist, *Mikhail Bakhtin* (Cambridge, MA: Harvard University Press, 1984), 206.

38. Clark and Holquist, *Mikhail Bakhtin*, 206.

152   *Christ Is the Question*

39. George Herbert Mead, *Mind, Self, and Society: From the Standpoint of a Social Behaviorist*, ed. & intro. by Charles W. Morris (Chicago: University of Chicago Press, 1934).

40. A good overview of recent work and prospective research in the social psychology of the self is provided by the collection of essays in *Self and Identity: Personal, Social, and Symbolic*, ed. Yoshihisa Kashima, Margaret Foddy, and Michael Platow (Mahwah, NJ: Lawrence Erlbaum Associates, 2002).

41. Hannah Arendt, quoted by Seyla Benhabib, *Situating the Self: Gender, Community, and Postmodernism in Contemporary Ethics* (Cambridge, England: Polity Press, 1992), 198.

Chapter 3

1. Cf. J. Louis Martyn, "We Have Found Elijah," in J. Louis Martyn, *The Gospel of John in Christian History: Essays, for Interpreters*, Theological Inquiries (New York: Paulist Press, 1978), 9–54.

2. See above, 45–46.

3. William S. Kurz, "The Function of Christological Proof from Prophecy for Luke and Justin" (PhD diss., Yale University, 1976), microform version: UMI 77–14048.

4. Among the scholars who quickly saw the significance of the biblical commentaries (*pesharim*) found at Qumran for understanding early Christian interpretation of Scripture, Nils A. Dahl was one of the most insightful. See especially his "Eschatology and History in Light of the Qumran Texts," in *Jesus the Christ: The Historical Origins of Christological Doctrine*, ed. Donald H. Juel (Minneapolis: Augsburg Fortress, 1991), 49–64, and other essays in this collection. "Sources of Christological Language," ibid., 113–36, provides a good summary of his work on our problem. For more recent work on the general question of biblical interpretation in the scrolls, see *Biblical Perspectives: Early Use and Interpretation of the Bible in Light of the Dead Sea Scrolls*, ed. Michael E. Stone and Esther G. Chazon, Studies on the Texts of the Desert of Judah (Leiden: Brill, 1998), 59–79.

5. Florentino García Martínez, *The Dead Sea Scrolls Translated: The Qumran Texts in English*, trans. Wilfred G. E. Watson (Leiden: E. J. Brill, 1994), 33.

6. Ibid., 200.

7. Ibid., 136.

8. Ibid., 13–14.

9. Ibid., 201, modified.

10. Schism: 1QpHab 2:1–10; 5:1–12; "Chaldaeans" = Kittim (Romans): 2:10–4:14; 5:12–6:12.

11. The relevant passages are *Jewish War* 2.117–18, 167–654; Book 3 as a whole deals with the revolt beginning in 66 CE; parallel accounts, written later, are in *Antiquities* 18–20.

12. The significance of these movements for understanding the context of early Christianity has been emphasized by Richard A. Horsley and John S. Hanson, *Bandits, Prophets, and Messiahs: Popular Movements in the Time of Jesus* (Minneapolis, Chicago, and New York: Winston, 1985), who interpret them through Eric Hobsbawm's neo-Marxist analysis of early modern and modern "bandits" and peasant uprisings. There is a huge literature on political aspects of the revolt; for context, E. Mary Smallwood, *The Jews under Roman Rule from Pompey to Diocletian: A Study in Political Relations* (Leiden: E. J. Brill, 1981), is unsurpassed; for a brief introduction, see David M. Rhoads, *Israel in Revolution: 6–74 C.E.: A Political History Based on the Writings of Josephus* (Philadelphia: Fortress, 1976).

13. Here again, an essay by Nils A. Dahl pinpoints the key issue: Nils Alstrup Dahl, "The Crucified Messiah," in *Jesus the Christ: The Historical Origins of Christological Doctrine*, ed. Donald H. Juel (Minneapolis: Fortress Press, 1991), 27–47. The essay was first published in German in 1960, in English in 1974.

14. The main point of Dahl, "Crucified Messiah."

15. This ritual interpretation of the death (and resurrection) is clearest in Paul's comments in Rom. 6:3–4.

16. The importance of the Psalms of Complaint in the formation of the early passion narratives has long been recognized; see, e.g., Donald Juel, *Messianic Exegesis: Christological Interpretation of the Old Testament in Early Christianity* (Philadelphia: Fortress, 1988), 89–117, with further references there.

17. Ibid., 77–81.

18. David M. Hay, *Glory at the Right Hand: Psalm 110 in Early Christianity*, SBL Monograph Series (Nashville: Abingdon, 1973); Juel, *Messianic Exegesis*, 135–50.

19. Alan F. Segal, *Two Powers in Heaven: Early Rabbinic Reports about Christianity and Gnosticism*, Studies in Judaism in Late Antiquity (Leiden: E. J. Brill, 1977).

20. Wayne A. Meeks, "The Image of the Androgyne: Some Uses of a

Symbol in Earliest Christianity," in Wayne A. Meeks, *In Search of the Early Christians: Selected Essays*, ed. Allen R. Hilton and H. Gregory Snyder (New Haven, CT, and London: Yale University Press, 2002), 3–54.

21. See, for example, James L. Kugel and Rowan A. Greer, *Early Biblical Interpretation*, Library of Early Christianity (Philadelphia: Westminster Press, 1986); Robert McQueen Grant and David Tracy, *A Short History of the Interpretation of the Bible* (Philadelphia: Fortress Press, 1984); P. R. Ackroyd and C. F. Evans, eds., *From the Beginnings to Jerome*, vol. 1 of *The Cambridge History of the Bible* (Cambridge: Cambridge University Press, 1975), 412–586.

Chapter 4

1. There is now a large literature about the practice of biblical interpretation in ancient Judaism. Among the most entertaining as well as insightful is James L. Kugel, *The Bible as It Was* (Cambridge, MA: Harvard University Press, 1997).

2. On Paul's unique uses of Scripture, Richard B. Hays, *Echoes of Scripture in the Letters of Paul* (New Haven, CT, and London: Yale University Press, 1989), is particularly illuminating.

3. Ronald F. Thiemann, "Radiance and Obscurity in Biblical Narrative," in *Scriptural Authority and Narrative Interpretation*, ed. Garrett Green (Philadelphia: Fortress Press, 1987), 21–41.

4. On the problems of converts reflected in 1 Thessalonians, see Abraham J. Malherbe, *Paul and the Thessalonians: The Philosophic Tradition of Pastoral Care* (Philadelphia: Fortress Press, 1987), 46–48, and also Wayne A. Meeks, *The Origins of Christian Morality: The First Two Centuries* (New Haven, CT, and London: Yale University Press, 1993), 18–36.

5. Margaret Mary Mitchell, *Paul and the Rhetoric of Reconciliation: An Exegetical Investigation of the Language and Composition of 1 Corinthians* (Louisville, KY: Westminster John Knox Press, 1992).

6. On the social situation in Corinth, see further Wayne A. Meeks, *The First Urban Christians: The Social World of the Apostle Paul*, 2nd ed. (New Haven, CT: Yale University Press, 2003), 47–49.

7. For more detailed analysis of Paul's moral strategy, see Wayne A. Meeks, "The Polyphonic Ethics of the Apostle Paul," in *In Search of the Early Christians: Selected Essays*, ed. Allen R. Hilton and H. Gregory Snyder (New Haven, CT, and London: Yale University Press, 2002), 196–209.

Chapter 5

1. Hans W. Frei, *Types of Christian Theology*, ed. George Hunsinger and William C. Placher (New Haven, CT, and London: Yale University Press, 1992), 139.
2. Frei, *The Eclipse of Biblical Narrative*.
3. Roland H. Bainton, *Here I Stand: A Life of Martin Luther* (New York: New American Library, Mentor, 1950), 144, citing the Weimar edition of Luther's works, 7:836–38.
4. Martin Luther, *On the Bondage of the Will*, conveniently translated along with the treatise by Erasmus, *On the Freedom of the Will*, in *Luther and Erasmus: Free Will and Salvation*, ed. and trans. E. Gordon Rupp and Philip S. Watson, Library of Christian Classics (Philadelphia: Westminster Press, 1969); Luther's response on the clarity of Scripture is on 158–69. See James Patrick Callahan, "*Claritas Scripturae*: The Role of Perspicuity in Protestant Hermeneutics," *Journal of the Evangelical Theological Society* 39, no. 3 (1996): 354.
5. See James Patrick Callahan, *The Clarity of Scripture: History, Theology, and Contemporary Literary Studies* (Downers Grove, IL: InterVarsity Press, 2001), and his article cited in the previous note.
6. The classic work by E. Harris Harbison, *The Christian Scholar in the Age of the Reformation* (Philadelphia: Porcupine Press, 1980), remains important on this topic.
7. See the very interesting remarks by Frei on "The Case of Berlin, 1810," in his *Types of Christian Theology*, 95–116.
8. Callahan, "*Claritas*," 367.
9. For a brief account of these developments, see Sydney Ahlstrom, *A Religious History of the American People* (New Haven, CT: Yale University Press, 1972), 429–54.
10. For a detailed analysis of the novels of Tim LaHaye and Jerry B. Jenkins, their culture, politics, and antecedents, see Glenn W. Shuck, *Marks of the Beast: The Left Behind Novels and the Struggle for Evangelical Identity* (New York: New York University Press, 2005).
11. A description of the Jesus Seminar and a brief sketch of its history may be found on its Web site, http://www.westarinstitute.org/Jesus_Seminar/jesus_seminar.html. It was founded in 1985 by Robert W. Funk, a New Testament scholar who has taught in several American universities and formerly served as executive secretary of the Society of Biblical Literature. For a clear but acerbic critique of the Seminar and related efforts, see Luke Timothy

Johnson, *The Real Jesus: The Misguided Quest for the Historical Jesus and the Truth of the Traditional Gospels* (San Francisco: HarperSan-Francisco, 1996).

12. See nn. 4 and 5 above.

13. Kathryn E. Tanner, "Theology and the Plain Sense," in *Scriptural Authority and Narrative Interpretation*, ed. Garrett Green (Philadelphia: Fortress Press, 1987), 59–78, quotations from 60, 72–74.

14. David H. Kelsey, *The Uses of Scripture in Recent Theology* (Philadelphia: Fortress, 1975).

15. On these questions, which seem at present especially to attract the attention of those who are most ready to declare the clarity of the Bible's moral teaching, see Wayne A. Meeks, "Biblical Perspectives: Homosexuality," *Christian Networks Journal*, Summer 2004, 46–48.

16. I tried to suggest something like this in my *The Origins of Christian Morality: The First Two Centuries* (New Haven, CT, and London: Yale University Press, 1993), 189–210.

17. George A. Lindbeck, *The Nature of Doctrine: Religion and Theology in a Post-Liberal Age* (Philadelphia: Westminster Press, 1984), 113–24.

18. Lindbeck acknowledges this, but in a deliberate oxymoron imagines an "open sect": George A. Lindbeck, "The Sectarian Future of the Church," in *The God Experience*, ed. Joseph P. Whelan (Westminster, MD: Newman, 1971), 226–43.

19. Maurice Wiles, "Scriptural Authority and Theological Construction: The Limitations of Narrative Interpretation," in *Scriptural Authority and Narrative Interpretation*, ed. Garrett Green (Philadelphia: Fortress Press, 1987), 42–58, quotations from 51–52.

20. Frei, *Types of Christian Theology*, 56, cf. 90.

21. From a letter to Thomas Butts, November 22, 1802, "Verses . . . composed . . . while Walking from Felpham to Lavant," lines 87–88.

22. Timothy Radcliffe, OP, *Talking to Strangers*, Woodward Lecture, Yale University, October 8, 1996 (n.p.: Privately printed, 1996).

Chapter 6

1. Frei tends to prefer the term "unsubstitutable," e.g., "The climax of the Gospel story is the full unity of the unsubstitutable individuality of Jesus with the presence of God" (Hans W. Frei, *The Identity of Jesus Christ: The Hermeneutical Bases of Dogmatic Theology*

[Philadelphia: Fortress Press, 1975], 154). On "unsurpassability," see also Lindbeck, *Nature of Doctrine*, 47–52.

2. See above, 119 and n. 20.

3. See above, 120f.

4. Lessing's 1779 play, *Nathan der Weise*, is a classic plea for religious tolerance, particularly among Jews, Christians, and Muslims: Gotthold Ephraim Lessing, *Nathan the Wise* (London: Nick Hern, 2003).

5. Mitchell, *Paul and the Rhetoric of Reconciliation*, 289 n. 580, referring to Chrysostom's *hom. in I Cor. 39.5–6.*

6. I have discussed this passage in greater detail in Wayne A. Meeks, "The Temporary Reign of the Son: 1 Cor 15:23–28," in *Texts and Contexts: Biblical Texts in Their Textual and Situational Contexts: Essays in Honor of Lars Hartman*, ed. Tord Fornberg and David Hellholm (Oslo, Copenhagen, Stockholm, and Boston: Scandinavian University Press, 1995), 801–11.

7. Paul W. Meyer, "Romans," in *The HarperCollins Bible Commentary*, ed. James L. Mays, rev. ed. (San Francisco: Harper, 2000), 1060.

8. I have treated this issue in greater detail in "On Trusting an Unpredictable God: A Hermeneutical Meditation on Romans 9–11," reprinted in my *In Search of the Early Christians*, 210–29.

9. Richard B. Hays, *Echoes of Scripture in the Letters of Paul* (New Haven, CT, and London: Yale University Press, 1989), 34–83.

Index of Modern Authors

Index of Subjects

affliction and joy, 89
ambition, 94
American Christianity, 4, 25
American culture, 3
American Jesus, 4
Anointed One, 77
   See also Messiah
anthropology, 19
anti-intellectualism, 111–12
apocalypses, 49
apocalypticism, 20, 49–52, 150
apologetic history, 69
archaeology, 47–48
Augustine, 2

Bakhtin, Mikhail, 57, 151
Baltimore Catechism, 36
baptism, 78, 81
Barth, Karl, 26–28
Bernard of Clairvaux, 38
Bible
   questions in, 2, 63
   Revised Standard Version, as "Red
      Bible," 146–47
   textual variants in, 11
boldness of speech, 90
Bonaventure, Saint, 10
"branch of David," 74
Bultmann, Rudolf Karl, 26–27, 49,
   150
Bultmann school, 28–30

Calvin, John, 109, 119
canon, 81, 116
Cartesian anxiety, 84
celebrity, 31
charisma, 94–95

Christ
   as slogan, 1–2
   unsurpassable, 23, 123–40
Christian character, formation of, 116
Christianity as proletarian movement,
   44
christological process, 75–76
christos. See Messiah
church and state, 37
circumcision, 91–92
cognitivist model of religion, 35–36,
   40
colonialism, 128
Confessing Church, 125
conflict in early Christianity, 52–53
conscience, liberation of, 32
conservatives and liberals, 32
conversion, 1–2, 92, 127–29
Corinth, Roman colony, 95
1 Corinthians, 93–94, 96–97, 99–100
Creed, Nicene, 4, 6, 142
creeds, 6
crucifixion, 85–87, 90
   as curse, 93
cultural incarnation, 4
cultural relativism, 20
culturally fashioned roles, 68

Da Vinci Code, The, 114
Damascus Covenant, 70
Darby, John Nelson, 113
Dead Sea Scrolls, 20, 22, 45–46, 51,
   69–74, 84, 149, 152
Debs, Eugene, 4
Deists, 13
demystifying the world, 33
Descartes, René, 16–17, 18, 20, 33

162